Reporting for Journalists

Reporting for Journalists explains the key skills needed by the news reporter. From the process of finding a story and tracing sources, to interviewing contacts, gathering information and filing the finished report, it is an essential handbook for students of journalism and a useful guide for working professionals.

Reporting for Journalists explores the role of the reporter in the world of modern journalism and emphasises the importance of learning to report across all media – radio, television, on-line, newspapers and periodicals. Using case studies, and examples of print and broadcast news stories, *Reporting for Journalists* includes:

- how to find a story and how to develop ideas

- researching the story and building the contacts book

- making best use of computer-aided reporting (CAR), newsgroups, chat rooms and search engines

- covering courts, councils and press conferences

- a chapter on broadcast reporting highlighting issues specific to television and radio

- an annotated guide to further reading, a glossary of key terms and a list of journalism web sites

Chris Frost is a principal lecturer in the Department of Journalism at the University of Central Lancashire. A journalist and a teacher for almost thirty years, he chairs the National Union of Journalists' ethics council. He is the author of *Media Ethics and Self-Regulation*.

Media Skills

SERIES EDITOR: RICHARD KEEBLE, CITY UNIVERSITY, LONDON
SERIES ADVISERS: WYNFORD HICKS AND JENNY MCKAY

The *Media Skills* series provides a concise and thorough introduction to a rapidly changing media landscape. Each book is written by media and journalism lecturers or experienced professionals and is a key resource for a particular industry. Offering helpful advice and information and using practical examples from print, broadcast and digital media, as well as discussing ethical and regulatory issues, *Media Skills* books are essential guides for students and media professionals.

Also in this series:

English for Journalists, 2nd edition
Wynford Hicks

Writing for Journalists
Wynford Hicks with Sally Adams and Harriett Gilbert

Interviewing for Radio
Jim Beaman

Producing for the Web
Jason Whittaker

Ethics for Journalists
Richard Keeble

Scriptwriting for the Screen
Charlie Moritz

Interviewing for Journalists
Sally Adams, with an introduction and additional material by Wynford Hicks

Researching for Television and Radio
Adèle Emm

Reporting for Journalists
Chris Frost

Find more details of current *Media Skills* books and forthcoming titles at **www.producing.routledge.com**

Reporting for Journalists

Chris Frost

ROUTLEDGE

Taylor & Francis Group

LONDON AND NEW YORK

Dedicated to the women in my life: my mother, wife, sister and daughters

First published 2002
by Routledge
11 New Fetter Lane, London EC4P 4EE

Simultaneously published in the USA and Canada
by Routledge
29 West 35th Street, New York, NY 10001

Routledge is an imprint of the Taylor & Francis Group

© 2001 Chris Frost
Chapter 10 © 2002 Cecile Wright

Typeset in Goudy Old Style and Syntax by Wearset Ltd, Boldon, Tyne and Wear
Printed and bound in Great Britain by Biddles Ltd, Guildford and King's Lynn

British Library Cataloguing in Publication Data
A catalogue record for this book is available from the British Library

Library of Congress Cataloging in Publication Data
Frost, Chris, 1950–
    Reporting for journalists / Chris Frost.
        p. cm. — (Media skills)
    Includes bibliographical references and index.
    1. Reporters and reporting. I. Title. II. Series.

PN4781 .F74 2001
070.4'3—dc21

                                                2001019945

ISBN 0-415-24087-5 (pbk.)
ISBN 0-415-24086-7 (hbk.)

Contents

1
Introduction

Some people want to become reporters for the glamour; some want to change the world. But I've always thought the best reporters do the job because they're just plain nosy. Holding up a mirror to society in order to present the truth is a laudable aim, but it is not always top priority when trying to hold together a newsdesk with limited resources and seemingly endless space to fill. The daily grind of filling pages is not always glamorous. But finding out what your community is up to because you can't stand not knowing, and then passing that knowledge on to help others manage their daily lives that little bit better, is rewarding and can be fun.

Journalism is the 'exercise by occupation of the right to free expression available to every citizen' (Robertson 1983: 3). There is nothing to stop anyone being a journalist, but in order to be paid for it you need to be able to do it better than most. This means finding stories people want to read, digging out as much as you can about them and getting the material back to your newsroom accurately and without delay. It's a tough brief, but an exciting one.

There can be few work-day thrills to match chasing a fire engine, gathering the story and then seeing your published piece on the front page complete with byline. The job satisfaction to be gained by spending days building a case against a corrupt politician, with all the careful meetings and research that involves, must also be hard to match in other careers. TV and radio journalists feel a similar thrill as their rushed but crafted pieces go on air with the quiet satisfaction of another job done to the best of their ability.

For someone who *needs* to know what is going on – who is endlessly fascinated by the doings of fellow humans – being a reporter is the perfect job. You are actually paid to gossip in pubs with shady characters, meet the rich and famous in an effort to find out how they got to be like that with only a little discernible talent, or expose the dirty doings of the lowlifes and criminals. It means that days are rarely the same and many lead to anecdotes that can keep veteran colleagues talking for hours in a cosy pub with the help of a few beers.

Of course not all reporters start as or want to be general news reporters and there are a number of specialists who get the same thrill from reporting on sport or cars or fashion or whatever it is that gets them excited.

Nearly every reporter in the UK these days starts his or her career on a journalism course. This will either be a one-year diploma course straight from school, a journalism degree or a postgraduate course following a degree in almost any subject. English, politics or media studies are popular choices. There are advantages to each type of course and every college varies in what it has to offer.

Those with a particular desire to be a political reporter, for instance, might be better off studying politics and then taking a postgraduate course in either broadcast or newspaper journalism. Those who are less certain where their future lies might prefer a journalism degree that will allow them to learn the business inside out.

It is probable that if you are reading this book, you are already on some sort of course, so it is not my intention to go into detail about the different types of courses. If you want to know more, then the National Council for the Training of Journalists, the Broadcast Journalism Training Council or the National Union of Journalists all offer sound advice. Their contact details, together with web addresses for some of the key courses in the UK, are at the back of the book.

I do think I should explain the range of jobs available within journalism. Most journalists start as reporters for local newspapers, radio stations or magazines. They cover general news, which means everything from police calls and chasing fire engines through to the local courts and councils. After a couple of years, a reporter will usually either start to specialise in a certain type of reporting, or will seek a news job on a larger paper or broadcast station, or both. It is also possible to move into the production side of newspapers to become a sub-editor or news executive. Promotion or career development usually involves moving to another town on another paper or station, or into London where a large number of the better-paid and more prestigious jobs are on offer.

This book is intended to guide student journalists towards good practice as they take their first steps towards becoming a reporter. I have tended to assume that your first job is, or will be, working for a local newspaper or radio station and so the advice is tailored for a local approach, although most of it applies to reporting at any level. Chapter 2 starts by looking at what a reporter is and what his or her role should be. It tries to explain what news is and the distinction that is made between news and feature material. Chapter 3 begins the process of finding a story and examines where reporters get stories from.

Chapter 4 gives advice on how to research the story. It looks at the sources reporters rely on and how to get in touch with them. It also considers computer-assisted reporting, an increasingly important field of expertise since the growth of the World Wide Web. In Chapter 5 the would-be reporter is shown how to work in a modern newsroom, while in Chapter 6 we go out on the road into an environment where self-reliance and initiative are the key to doing a great job. Going out on the road is a waste of time unless you are contacting people and so Chapter 7 is all about who to see and how to deal with them. Chapter 8 takes us inside the door to cover court, council and press conferences; dealing with a wide range of contacts and considering who to see, where to go and what to do.

Having arranged your interview, you need to question your source, and Chapter 9 covers the important points of carrying out a good interview for news reporting. Broadcast reporters have some special problems that do not effect newspaper or magazine reporters and in Chapter 10, Cecile Wright, a highly-experienced BBC radio and TV reporter and journalism lecturer, discusses the solutions and explains how to work with a recorder and/or crew. She considers how best to use sound and pictures, actuality and interviews, and think about location/studio links and pieces to camera. There's no point having the best story in the world if you can't get it back to the newsdesk, so Chapter 11 explains how to file the story. Copy filing by computer or phone is the norm these days, but you still need to know how to present copy on paper. Modern technology can add extra pressure during a breaking story and again there is sound advice on how to do this with the least amount of stress. Too many reporters think that filing the story is the end of a good job, but those whose careers really take off know that it's what happens next that marks out the really good reporter. Chapter 12 shows you how to spin several articles/features out of the same idea. It tells you how to become your editor's favourite reporter, the one who can always be relied upon to provide great copy with feature spin offs, picture ideas and new stories. Chapter 13 brings the book to a close with a bibliography, a recommended book list, useful web sites, and advice about where to find codes of practice and how to contact useful journalism organisations.

I hope that you enjoy the book and that it helps you to go on to work at something that you will find to be worthwhile, lots of fun and that offers much career satisfaction.

2
The role of the reporter

What is a reporter and how does the good reporter relate to the world? A good reporter is unavoidably linked with what society sees as important about journalism. Many claims are made about the importance of journalism in a modern democracy. That great *Times* editor Delane believed:

> The duty of the journalist is the same as that of the historian – to seek out the truth, above all things, and to present to his readers not the truth as statecraft would wish them to know, but the truth as near as he can attain it.
>
> (cited in Williams 1957: 8)

Randall believes something similar and says that good journalists wherever they are will be attempting the same thing: 'intelligent fact-based journalism, honest in intent and effect, serving no cause but the discernible truth, and written clearly for its readers whoever they may be' (1996: 2).

Franklin on the other hand is more sceptical and says of Randall: 'These are giddy claims which will doubtless trigger incredulity among many readers of the contemporary British press' (Franklin 1997: 29). Franklin believes the view of journalists as fearless crusaders and journalism as an investigative activity requires qualification. He also points out that, willingly or not, journalists do occasionally print untruths or half-truths.

This is the reporter's dilemma. We know that much is expected of us in terms of gathering the truth and presenting it to a public that supports the ideals of individual liberty and democratic government, but we also know that the reality is usually driven by money and profit.

It's like mixing up politicians with politics. Politics is about democracy and the right of people to have their views considered by those in power. Most politicians support this view – they probably even believe it – but when it actually comes to putting it into practice, things are rarely so high-minded.

Politicians are ambitious and human, just like everyone else, and just like us they want to be popular and they want to be re-elected. This means they often try to hide their mistakes or prevent us making full and informed choices by limiting the information they make available to the democratic process. Journalists can hardly claim to be any different. We all try to get by as honestly as we can, but the need to make a living can tempt us all to bend our principles.

Much of journalism is the routine gathering of information, most of it predictable and based around such events as court hearings, council meetings, sporting events and parliament. These days, with the pursuit of media consumers more crucial than ever before, the journalist has also had to become entertainer, finding stories and features that will delight the audience rather than inform, titillate rather than educate. With ever-increasing media output tempting audiences to spend less and less time with any individual provider, persuading readers to spend a little longer with your newspaper has become one of the critical performance measures for the media. Consequently journalists rarely get the time or the encouragement for the big investigation to expose corruption or right wrongs. They are required to find entertaining and exciting stories quickly and with minimum research. Rather than investigate the detailed rights and wrongs of a major political debate, they will report only the 'row' between the major protagonists. This kind of reporting has the confrontation, drama and, of course, entertainment value of the gladiatorial contests of the Roman era without the blood and gore, but helps no-one to understand the issues in what might be an important political debate.

Both the *News of the World* and *Tonight with Trevor MacDonald* used the parents of Sarah Payne, cruelly killed in the summer of 2000 while on holiday, to support stories calling for a 'Megan's law' in Britain. Megan's law, which requires the US police to notify neighbourhoods in which a sexual predator comes to live, is highly controversial. Paedophile sexual predators have become one of the major moral panics of the 1990s and early part of the twenty-first century. The crime is seen as so abnormal and horrific that the perpetrators can be condemned without explanation as monsters, while the solution seems simple. Very little has been written about how to prevent people becoming predators in the first place because it is very time consuming and difficult and, in any case, is not what people want to read. Far easier to report on the demands for Megan's law which only requires a few quotes from suitably emotive sources. Randall, Delane and others may not like it, but tirelessly rooting out the entire truth on a story of this sort is very expensive and the sorts of news organisations that can afford it do not sell in the markets that would want to read it.

Some journalists would claim that this in-depth investigation is not really news reporting, while the Paynes' calling for a Megan's law in Britain is. But this is just semantics. News might be the topical edge of the story and features the softer core, but it is all about journalism and truth-seeking. The Thalidomide investigation by the *Sunday Times* of the 1970s was a large-scale investigation run over a long period by a relatively large team, and is widely regarded as one of British journalism's finest hours. *Death on the Rock* was an award-winning documentary that required an immense amount of investigation and earned the searing wrath of the then-Prime Minister, Margaret Thatcher. This is also widely agreed to be one of the high peaks of journalistic endeavour. It can be done; it just isn't done very often and is being done less and less. It's much more profitable to offer the latest gossip on Posh and Becks to a large audience than to sell a week-long investigation into corruption.

This also applies to TV, which is facing similar problems to newspapers. Increasing numbers of channels, competition from satellite and cable channels and the move to digital has made TV in the UK much more competitive and, say many critics, has forced it to dumb down.

Of course much of our view of the reporter as investigative crusader is, in any case, drawn from the world of entertainment rather that reality. It is somewhat ironic that we have people trying to claim that the only real reporters are ones who are probably only fictional in the first place.

Journalists such as Clark Kent and Lou Grant and a host of others from cinema or TV fight the good fight, often on a weekly basis. But in reality, it is the daily routine of news stories that are the journalist's bread and butter.

REPORTING IN DIFFERENT MEDIA

A reporter of 50 years ago started work in newspapers and, after a career of several years in weekly and daily journalism, had to decide whether to move into the growing area of broadcast or stay in newspapers.

It is no longer such a straightforward decision. Broadcasting and now on-line media are fast becoming the way forward for reporting. Newspapers are likely to be published into the foreseeable future and magazines will be with us for a long time to come, but electronic publishing is becoming more important every day. Most modern reporters need to learn a range of skills that will allow them to work in different media throughout their career.

There are obvious differences working in the different media, but there are more similarities that might originally be supposed.

All the media require reporters with the same basic qualifications:

- an overwhelming curiosity about people and events;

- dogged determination to find out what is going on;

- an ability to mix with people, charm them and persuade them to tell you things;

- an ability to come up with interesting and original ideas for news stories and features;

- the initiative and cunning to get to places and people;

- the ability to present the information gathered in a way that suits the medium and the target audience.

Whilst the technology for the different media separates the practitioners, the common elements above mean that whatever the discipline, a reporter feels a common bond with other reporters. Learning to work with a camera team; coming to terms with the limitations of text; presenting stories that do not allow you to use any pictures or, indeed, working with a medium that allows you to use text, sound, pictures and video but that places impossible demands in terms of a deadline and the breadth of material it will swallow, are all problems that the reporter must quickly come to terms with.

Television

TV reporters need to have a real awareness of image and the way that pictures will affect the story. They are less concerned with literature and are more concerned with emotion and good pictures. This can mean they are often more concerned with the way sources present the material than what is actually said, but it can also mean putting over powerful messages.

Radio

Radio journalists do not need to think in pictures, but they do need to be able to paint pictures with sound. Sound is a very important medium because its approach is much more direct. We can concentrate on driving, for instance, but still listen to a radio broadcast. We can't (or most of us can't) concentrate on reading a newspaper and still do other tasks. Radio is a very immediate medium and is probably the best at alerting the public to a news story. Presentation is important in radio, because vocal tone is very important in radio work. Someone with an irritating voice or a strong accent or dialect would not find radio work easy.

Print

Print journalists are able to gather more on a story and are generally able (or often required) to gather more stories. The newspaper is still (with the exception of on-line) the medium with the most amount of space to lavish on appropriate stories. Filling space is much more likely to be a problem for the newspaper reporter than for broadcasters. Many a district office reporter on one of the big evening papers faces the daily task of filling two pages of news on his or her own. This leaves little time for investigation or thinking about presentation. The newspaper reporter still needs to be creative about stories, however, and needs to think about picture ideas.

On-line

It's probably too early to tell what sort of reporter makes a good on-line reporter. Indeed, at this stage, there are not many on-line reporters at all. There are plenty of on-line journalists, but they are more likely to be receiving material gathered for one of the more traditional media and sent on for an on-line news site.

NEWS: WHAT IT IS AND HOW TO IDENTIFY IT

The media is there to present the consumer with information, whether that is a review, news report, feature, profile or listings of forthcoming events. Even the adverts contain some information. You need to understand what it is that people want to read or hear on their news bulletins if you are to make a good reporter.

Although many reporters write news and features, you need to have a clear awareness of the difference so that you can understand how to use different techniques in different types of story.

We all, as human beings, seem to require information in order to function, and there seem to be two types of information that we are particularly interested in. The first tells us about our surroundings and environment; information that we need in order, at the basest level, to ensure our survival. We need to predict where we are likely to find food and where we are likely to find safe shelter. Of course, in a modern world, our desires are much more sophisticated and so our intelligence gathering is directed towards our pockets, our comfort and our security.

The second type of information is about ourselves and, by extension, our fellow human beings. Most people want to be considered normal members of their society (or subset of society) – to fit in and be accepted, and they are prepared to modify their behaviour to do this. In small communities, hundreds of years ago, we could do that by observation. But in large, educated, metropolitan, even global communities, it is much more difficult. It is even possible to be a member, or want to be a member, of a subset of society where your physical contact with similar members is limited to two or three people in the local community. The Internet has proved to be a powerful force in normalising such small sub-societies and it is likely this development will continue. The traditional media thought has always been a normalising influence, allowing *Telegraph* readers (for instance) to commune with other *Telegraph* readers and accept and adjust shared values no matter where they live in the country.

As the world has become more sophisticated, so it has become more difficult to align such shared values and it is here that the media has had an important part to play. We now get our views about society from sources such as soap operas, dramas, the news, news features and true-life tales in magazines and web site fanzines.

One of the difficulties we have is separating fact from fiction. We need to be able to work out that our favourite soap opera might well have something to say about how British society works, whereas a drama such as the *X-Files*, popular though it may be, perhaps doesn't. This is even more important in news, where we are relying on accurate, timely information for more immediate support in areas such as our comfort and security. We need to be able to separate fact from rumour, truth from propaganda.

The communities to which we belong are very important to us because we like to belong and we enjoy the companionship of those with whom we feel comfortable. Most of us belong to a number of overlapping social groupings in which we hold greater or lesser positions of social status such as the following:

- family;
- friends (often based around school or work);
- local special interest group;
- school, college or work;
- home town;
- hobby or leisure activity;
- profession, work group or trade union;
- nation.

Many of these groupings hold their community interest with gossip. It is for this reason that we should not be surprised that gossip plays an important part of news reporting, particularly in newspapers which have been overtaken by radio and TV as an alerting medium. No-one really uses newspapers nowadays to follow a breaking story. TV and radio are far better at it. But newspapers are good at gossip, which relies on small but significant details.

Gluckman says that gossip can also be used by social groups to preserve their exclusiveness by closing the doors to parvenus (Gluckman 1963). Many of the society gossip columns use this effect to be open enough to allow readers to understand, but not be part of an exclusive set that they wish to join. Gossip is often described as 'soft news'; news about people and their relationships. It is news in which we are interested, but are often scornful about.

'Hard news' is easier to justify. Any new or threatening situation may require us to make decisions and this requires information. So important is communication during a disaster that normal social barriers are often lowered. We will talk to strangers in a way we would never consider normally. Even relatively low grade disruption of our life such as a fire drill or a very late train seems to give us the permission to breach normal etiquette and talk to strangers. The more important an event to a particular public, the more detailed and urgent the requirement for news becomes. Without an authoritative source of facts, whether that is a newspaper or trusted broadcast station, rumours often run riot. Rumours start because people believe their group to be in danger and so, although the rumour is unverified, feel they should pass it on. For example, if a worker heard that their employer's business was doing badly and people were going to be made redundant, they would pass that information on to colleagues.

According to Tamotsu Shibutani (1966) rumour is a group process. Groups of people discuss a piece of information one of them has heard and then pass that on to others together with their own interpretation. That interpretation might include their own knowledge, their own fears and their own concerns. All of these might alter the rumour, changing it from the original story. Journalists are often dragged into the rumour machine and this could be when a story first claims a reporter's attention.

A reporter always needs to play the sceptic, listening, but demanding proof and seeking sources. Sometimes the story is too good to risk not using as quickly as possible. This means checking as much as possible and then following up the detail for later editions or bulletins.

Tamotsu Shibutani (1966) hypothesises that if the demand for news in a public exceeds the supply made available through institutional channels, rumour construction is likely to occur. We see this happening when a big story breaks and demand for news exceeds its supply because reporters simply cannot gather enough material quickly enough to satisfy demand and interest (Frost 2000: 20). This certainly happened following the death of the Princess of Wales in 1997. Social barriers were lowered and strangers talked openly about the death in trains and buses. People were desperate to find out more information and rumours ran riot.

At its most simple, news is information we were unaware of until we read it or saw it in the media. However, much news is predictable, keeping us up to date with stories we know to be happening. News can be said to be a *factual* (the reporter should have gone to considerable pains to ensure the material is truthful), *topical* event that is *of interest to the target group* of the media outlet producing it. The Royal Commission on the Press (1949) (The Ross commission) said about news:

> There are, however, certain elements common to all conceptions of news. To be news an event must first be interesting to the public, and the public for this purpose means for each paper the people who read that paper, and others like them. Second, and equally important, it must be new, and newness is measured in newspaper offices in terms of minutes.
>
> (1949: 103)

The commission went on to identify items of interest as being: sport; news about people; news about strange or amusing adventures; tragedies; accidents; crimes; 'News whose sentiment or excitement brings some colour into life' (ibid.: 104).

The commission used *new* in the sense in which I use *topical*: it has happened within the frequency of the medium in which it appears. So for a weekly paper, it is anything that has happened within that week; for a radio bulletin, it is anything that has happened since the last bulletin. Nowadays we talk about target groups to mean what the Ross commission described as 'the people who read that paper and others like them' (ibid.).

Which stories interest a target group is a matter of judgment. Alastair Hetherington, editor of the *Guardian* in the 1960s, drew up a list of priorities for new staff:

- significance: social, economic, political;

- drama: excitement, entertainment;

- surprise: unpredictability, newness;

- personalities: royalty, showbiz;

- sex, scandal, crime;

- numbers: scale of the event;

- proximity: its geographical closeness (cited in Venables 1993: 3).

Johan Galtung and Mari Ruge were amongst the first academics to try to understand news decision making in a study first published in the 1960s. They saw news broken down into two categories: general news value and news values of particular importance to Western media. They identified the time elements and the need to coincide news choices with the perceived audience. They also identified that the media favoured news that directly affected the target audience or was easy for the target audience to understand, that there tended to be a news threshold and that space limitations varied that threshold (Galtung and Ruge 1997).

Journalists tend to use stories with clear time frames (disasters, crime, political rows) and if stories are about important issues but have no clear start time and no clear development highlights, they will try to provide one. So, for instance, rather than carry a story about hospital waiting lists and what is being done (or not done) about them, it is easier to print stories about the government's latest claim to be doing something or the opposition's claim that they are failing, as this gives a clearly identifiable time frame.

Hetherington identifies news from experience, while Galtung and Ruge identify it from observation, but they were not able to give clear rules that we could apply in any situation. Philip Schlesinger (1978: 51) reminds us that the problems of *time constraints* and *logistics* will also have an effect on whether a story makes it to the news bulletins. Logistical problems may, for instance, lead journalists to produce stories closer to home rather than spend time, money and effort taking a film crew abroad. If they do need to go abroad, they are more likely to justify the expense by filing stories that are well below the normal threshold. Did you notice for instance how many stories we got from Australia while all those media people were in Sydney to cover the Olympics? Western media is inevitably drawn towards covering elite nations because of the ability to travel quickly and easily and use the fast communication methods in the West.

John Venables is another thinker about news. He comes to the conclusion that *change* and *security concern* are 'two fundamental factors which motivate attentiveness in an audience' (Venables 1993: 34). He goes on to describe the importance of change: 'Without change, information cannot be interpreted as news. Change is important because it involves uncertainty, which in turn generates attention and concern' (ibid.). Change is undoubtedly a defining parameter of our lives. We measure time by changes. We wake up and go to work (a change); we stop work for lunch (a change); and so on. This is why some days seem boring and others fly by – it all depends on the amount of change. Change also explains why we choose a particular time to write about a certain story. The events roll like a river but there has to be a reason why we build the news story at a particular point on the bank. That point is usually a change where a definite action may have been made, a decision taken. This change turns the otherwise continuously-flowing story into news. It is worth noting that journalists and PR people often 'manufacture' stories by artificially inserting a change, such as ringing a source and then leading on the comments that source made. Venables also identifies *familiarity* (ibid.) as an important constituent of news. Galtung and Ruge before him saw *unambiguity* and *consonance* (1997) as important components of news. These terms mean that news stories will have a cultural basis that is understood by the audience so that explanation is kept to a minimum. Reporters covering the US 2000 presidential elections for the UK had to spend much time explaining the US electoral system so that the UK audience could understand why the story was so significant. If the election had been from a country of lesser significance, they probably would not have bothered. So, any news editor making a choice of news stories will be looking for stories that are:

- *topical* (fits within the time frame and involves a *change*);

- *true* (or at least have some basis in truth);

- are fit for the *target* group. For this they need to be *familiar*, but involve *change*, and be of interest to the group.

These may, of course, be constrained by *logistics* and possibly *composition*. Composition was identified by Galtung and Ruge (1997) and suggests that a story might be used because of the type of news elsewhere on the page or in the bulletin. One would not want a bulletin that was all politics for instance, and so a crime story might make it to the bulletin even though it is not very strong. ITN's 'and finally' stories were ideal examples of composition. The stories were set to a pattern and designed to end the bulletin on a positive note. They were not chosen for their news value, but to fit into the composition structure of the bulletin.

SPECIALIST REPORTING

A number of people become reporters for the consumer and trade magazine industries, because they are specialists in their fields rather than because they are journalists. They work with journalists and what they produce can be considered journalism, but they might still describe themselves as something else. Academics and some other professionals are particularly prone to follow this route. Whether they are lawyers, doctors, technologists, engineers or chemists, they are writing about their subject, popularising for ordinary people. Sports personalities and entertainers also join this throng of writers producing specialist columns, often for a specialist press market.

But there are also a number of journalists who, having served their apprenticeship as a news reporter, want to move on to specialist areas of writing. Sport is always a popular choice but showbiz, motoring, crime, politics and fashion are other areas that attract enthusiastic specialists who write with deep knowledge for their newspapers or broadcast with passion for TV or radio. These specialists need all the basic skills of the reporter. They must be able to identify a good story. They need to be able to develop ideas to create further news stories or features. They must be able writers or broadcasters. In addition, they must have a passion for their chosen specialism and a desire to learn much more about it. That desire usually turns them into considerable experts after a few years.

Many of the specialists have their own clubs and there is the wine-writers' circle, a motor-writers' guild, a football writers' association and so on.

3
Finding a story

As Mrs Beaton might have it: first find your story. No newspaper or news bulletin would sell without stories and it is the reporter's job to find them. Much news can be anticipated and is the routine of daily life. These diary stories are tracked by the newsdesk and allocated to the reporter. These can be anything from a flower show to a United Nations press conference. Whatever the event, they all share one thing in common – someone wants you to cover the event and print stories about it. The flower show organiser wants local people to know about the show and its winners, the United Nations conference is to tell the world of some new initiative and enhance the reputation of the UN. Stories that are not pre-ordained are often more interesting. The *off-diary* story is one discovered by the reporter on his/her own initiative and is often a story someone somewhere doesn't want covered, whether it is the Hamiltons' stay in the Paris Ritz, or the local mayor's illegal drug habit. Diary stories are the bread and butter of most local newspapers and radio stations – but it is the off-diary story that interests the good reporter and it is a mark of status within the newsroom to be taken off the diary and allowed to work completely on one's own initiative.

MARKET CONSIDERATIONS

The first thing a reporter needs to consider when finding a story is the market. If you are working for a local weekly paper then the stories you choose, how you approach them and how you write them will be very different to those on the local radio or on the national news.

The audiences of Radio 4, the *Daily Telegraph* and the *Sun* are all different, as are the audiences of *Cosmopolitan* and the *Burnley Express*, although with the right presentation, all those publications might be interested in the same story.

You need to know the target audience well to make decisions about the use of a story. The more the target audience is interested, the keener the editor will be to use the story, and the more copy he or she will require. This is possibly even more important if you are working as a freelance. A good freelance knows at a glance which publication/broadcast outlet will be interested in which story, how much material they would want on it and how to angle the story. If you produce stories suitable for the *Sun* but try to sell them to BBC national news, or vice versa, you will soon go broke.

Most national newspapers, magazines and broadcast outlets these days have very clear ideas about exactly who their publication is aimed at. This is a little more difficult on the local scene, where the temptation is to aim at everybody in the geographic area. However, most newspapers and local radio stations have a type of person in mind when writing or broadcasting. Local independent radio for instance tries to attract the 15–24-year-old market with short news bulletins and the latest pop music, while BBC local radio with its greater emphasis on talk, is more likely to aim at the 50-year-old+ audience. Radio and particularly TV have only relatively short bulletins and so can only choose the most important news for the audience. A national TV news bulletin can only carry the amount of news that would fit on a national newspaper's front page and the presentation order and choice is often determined by the quality of the supporting video. Newspapers need to attract on the news-stand and so will attempt a unique selling point if possible. The *Daily Mail*, for instance, aims at middle-class, middle-aged women with aspirations. Much of its news concerns issues that are directly connected with its readers' lives such as education (most have children at school or college), the work place or crime or is lifestyle-based, looking at fashion, consumerism and the lives of the rich and famous. This *ethnocentric* nature of news (Watson 1998: 106) means that news is never the direct reflection of society that some commentators would have us believe, such as Randall, when he wrote of holding 'up a mirror to society, reflecting its virtues and vices and also debunking its cherished myths' (Randall 1996: 2). A more accurate description might be the mirror of the fairy tale evil stepmother: 'Mirror, mirror on the wall, who is the fairest of them all?' It is not a mirror at all but wish fulfilment. The media all too often is there to tell people what they want to hear.

News is aimed at an audience – an audience that, in most cases, has to be persuaded to buy the product. Audiences are not passive things that lap up all they are given – they are selective and choose which items of media they buy according to their enjoyment or need for what is on offer. This means that news is bound to follow certain patterns that the good reporter learns to identify: 'all news is reported from some particular angle' (Fowler 1999: 10).

DIARY STORIES

Diary stories (or on-diary stories as they are sometimes known) are notified to the newsdesk from a number of external sources and are entered in the diary. A show here, a press conference there, everything from a local council meeting to a charity ball will be entered into the diary and may be allocated to a reporter to cover. It is important that any event you learn of is entered in the diary so that the news editor is also aware of it. It may well be an event you are unable to cover personally. You should also note follow-up ideas in the diary. For instance, if a local school is campaigning to build a new sports hall, then you should note all the key dates of the campaign in the diary to remind yourself and the newsdesk to follow up their progress. Local courts and council meetings are still a staple of the local paper. But there are plenty of other routine events that are entered in the diary year after year.

Press releases

The most common source of stories, certainly on local papers and local radio stations, is the press release. These have grown in importance over the last twenty years as editorial staffs in many provincial papers have been reduced and more and more organisations have become media sensitive. A local weekly paper that, during the 1970s, had an editorial staff of ten might now struggle by with five. There are a number of reasons for this. Franklin and Murphy identify seven significant factors (Franklin and Murphy 1998: 9). Whatever the reasons, newsdesks are now more likely to use press releases from local businesses, societies, sports clubs and am-dram groups than ever before.

Try to remember that hand-outs are a propaganda vehicle for the sender. No-one sends a press release which shows them, their company or group in a bad light. You must read between the lines to get at the real story and you may need to ring the contact for further information. Some press releases of course are absolutely straightforward and just need to be presented in a tight, bright style. In my spare time I'm a publicity officer on a local gala committee. This means I send press releases about the festival day to the local media. The releases are straightforward information about the gala that will interest local people and are written in an appropriate style with quotes from the chairman of the committee. Not surprisingly, these are usually used in their entirety and uncut by the local papers. Only if they want more, do they tend to come back to me seeking extra quotes or picture ideas.

Other news outlets

Other newspapers or broadcast stations are a good source of news. Competing papers and magazines and the national papers need to be read every day so that stories that may have a link to your target audience can be followed up. Radio and television needs to be monitored constantly for the same reason. This is why so many media outlets all seem to zero in on the same story. One outlet carries the story and others then feel it is important enough for them to follow up.

Advertisements

Advertisements often carry good stories, particularly for regional papers and radio stations. Births, marriages and deaths (BMDs), unusual job vacancies, strange items for sale or offbeat public announcements can often lead to good stories. Public announcements from councils are also a good source of stories as they will often signal plans for major developments or changes. Any news-desk worth its salt will arrange with the advertising department to give them a sight of BMDs and public announcements as early as possible in the day.

Anniversaries

Anniversaries are an easy source of good stories allowing you to relive the event using archive pictures, video or sound. Interviews with those involved a year, ten years or even twenty years on can provide good human interest features, news stories or current affairs programmes. All of us enjoy reminiscing and these features give us the chance to say 'Is it really a year since . . . ?'. Such features also allow the passage of time to add perspective to a story.

Academe

Academics and academic journals can be good sources of stories, particularly for specialist correspondents. Many an academic is desperate to make a reputation and will happily talk about their latest research. Whilst the number of academic journals available can be daunting, the Internet now allows a notification of when journals in which you are interested are published and what they contain. Many journals or the articles in them are too dry by far to be of interest to a general readership, but reporters on specialist magazines or health or education correspondents do find the occasional nugget tucked away in the likes of the *British Medical Journal*, the *Lancet* or one of the science journals. The story of whether the MMR vaccine given to children to protect against mumps, measles and rubella causes autism has been raging for several years now and is occasionally stoked up when a scientist publishes a paper that claims to shed light on the issue.

Official sources

Council minutes and agendas, government press releases and court lists are often sources of good stories. Careful reading of the detail (budget cuts, odd purchases or personnel changes) can often lead to good stories. Once, years ago, when reading the Social Services Committee minutes of a local authority, I realised that the figures listing the number of children taken into care each year and the number put into children's homes compared with the number sent to foster homes, meant that the vast majority of children, more than 80 per cent, were sent straight back home to live with their natural parents despite being taken into local authority care as being in danger. We were able to run the stories for weeks across the front and inside pages. Many councillors leapt on the bandwagon to make it a great story. I'd like to be able to say we completely changed the way children were dealt with, but of course we didn't. But we did force some people to treat the situation more seriously.

Parliament is also now much more accessible, with Hansard and all the current Bills and Acts of Parliament available on the web. Any political correspondent needs to make regular visits here. Government press releases are also available on-line. You can often spin a good local story from a national government press release (see www.coi.gov.uk).

OFF-DIARY STORIES

Off-diary stories are more difficult to come by. These require the reporter to be more creative, thinking up ways to track down stories that are not going to be notified to the newsdesk. It means keeping your eyes and ears open for unusual happenings.

Observation

It is vital that the keen reporter keeps his or her eyes open all the time. Many stories come from spotting people behaving oddly. The gathering of crowds is always a sign that something is happening, and you need to find out what is attracting them. Sirens are another indicator. Find out where the noise is coming from and get there quick, but try to remember that some factories still use sirens to signify knocking-off time! Changes in buildings, demolitions, site clearances, posters, planning application notifications and unusual signs can all lead to good stories.

Eaves-dropping

Eaves-dropping is usually condemned as rude, but a good reporter is interested in everything and sometimes can't help over-hearing interesting conversations or seeing something out of the ordinary. If the overheard conversation seems to contain something that would make a good story, it seems to me that the good reporter should immediately identify him or herself to the speakers: 'Excuse me, I'm ... a reporter with the *Bexley Bugle*. I couldn't help overhearing what you just said and I wondered if you would tell me more about it ...'. There might, of course, be exceptions to that. If what is taking place is criminal or seriously against the public interest, then it might be important to gather the information and keep your identity secret. You would then need to make an effort to find out who the speakers were. For instance, imagine you had heard a councillor and a local builder discussing what was obviously some form of corruption. Exposing such corruption would be in the public interest and introducing yourself would serve no purpose except to alert the speakers. You would need to find out who they were (some councils issue pictures of local councillors or you will have pictures in your library) and then track down the evidence to back up the overheard conversation.

Personal contacts

Every reporter lives by his or her contacts – it marks the difference between a good reporter and a great reporter. A great reporter knows people from all walks of life. No matter what is happening, they will know someone who can tell them all about it – or at the very least give them the name of someone else who can tell them all about it. Radio and TV journalists often get stories from listeners and viewers who call in, building on the perceived relationship they have with this regular visitor to their front rooms. This relationship with the reporter is important. Newspapers have picked up on this and many news-papers now use picture bylines in an attempt to build up a relationship with the reader, so that they will feel more inclined to contact the reporter. Some national papers byline with the reporter's e-mail address so that readers can interact better with the story. National TV news bulletins regularly add their e-mail address or promote their web sites.

It is important that a good journalist should have as wide a range of contacts as possible at local, regional and national level. This ensures that you can provide different levels of sourcing for any story.

Community groups

Charitable and voluntary groups are an important part of any local commun-ity. Whether it is a local charity, the Scouts or Guides, a church group or a social society, these are local people doing what interests them in the community and some of it at least can be turned into news or features. Many editors like to have reporters assigned to a section of the circulation area in order to get in touch with such groups. Any such reporter needs to contact the secretaries of local community groups, the local church ministers, head teachers, post offices, libraries, publicans and others central to the life of the community. Many places such as doctors' surgeries, libraries, post offices and shops carry adverts and notices of the minutiae of community life and these also need to be checked.

CALLS

Calls are one of the standard jobs in any newsroom. This involves calling the police, fire service and ambulance service to see whether they have been involved in any newsworthy incidents. Daily papers tend to contact the services three or four times a day. Radio and TV keep in touch even more often. Weekly papers can make do with one contact per day. In some areas, the emergency services have become so bogged down with dealing with the calls that they have instituted an automated system. They record the calls for the day and local news services listen to a recorded message, only going to the press office if more information is required. This allows the press office in that emergency service to concentrate on gathering the information and answering specific questions.

ETHICAL CONSIDERATIONS

There are, inevitably, some ethical considerations when tracking down stories. I've already mentioned eaves-dropping, but there are other things as well. Often journalists are invited into people's offices or homes to gather information. It seems to me an invasion of privacy to take the opportunity to rifle through their drawers or papers or look at documents in their computer while they've popped off to make a cup of coffee or visit the toilet. Reading someone's private papers or their mail must surely be wrong. Having said that, being able to read upside down is a useful technique – searching for material is one thing, reading it another.

Plagiarism

Plagiarism is the offence of copying someone else's work. This is identified as unprofessional by the NUJ and is generally considered to be wrong. Apart from anything else, you cannot be sure that the tempting story that appears in the opposition paper is right.

You might use such a story as a tip off and even contact the person named in the story to get further details, but you need to get your own version. This gives you the chance to update the information, fish around for additional information and approach other contacts for support. Of course it would be perfectly legitimate to say that such and such a paper or TV bulletin has reported that something has happened.

MORE THAN WORDS

These days, it is not enough to think solely about the story and how it could be presented in words. If you are working for TV or radio, it is obvious that pictures and sound will also be required, but even for newspapers pictures are important and the Internet requires pictures, audio and video.

Pictures

Good pictures can make a story. In the TV age, the ability to illustrate stories is paramount. Pictures can add emotion and authenticity. Whilst no-one these days is foolish enough to believe the camera never lies, pictures can add a lot of detail and a sense of authenticity to a story. A picture can add context, explain what is happening, allow us to identify someone or allow us to classify someone or a group of people. It also allows us to see the non-verbal communication (NVC) in the picture and start to add our own meanings to what is happening. Lacey (1998: 11) lists facial expression, gaze, gestures, posture, body contact and clothes and appearance as all being forms of NVC (1998: 12) that can add strength to the story in a way words cannot.

You need to think about pictures on every story you cover. Of course for TV, this is so vital it is central to everything you are doing. Some photographer (or camera crews) take briefings better than others, but all of them need to know what the story is about and the ideas you have had for photographs. This could be as simple as a portrait to illustrate a news item or feature about a personality. On a more complex story you might need to explain to the photographer what it is you are hoping to achieve and how. On a major incident such as a plane crash, you will probably need to let the photographer loose to take action pictures as they happen while you attend the press conferences and try to find out what has happened. Only later might you suggest pictures of specific people or places.

Audio

Audio is as vital for radio as video is for TV, and you need to consider carefully how you add audio effects. Background sound can add authenticity to a story. Interviewing a railway spokesperson on the platform with the noise of announcements, customers and trains needs to be handled with care from a technical point of view but says much about trains and passengers that would be difficult to get into the interview any other way. Beware of background noise of effects that detract from the story. A story about traffic congestion with the country sounds of bird calls and insect noise, rather than the growl of queuing motors, would sound peculiar. Radio likes to tell the story through the people being interviewed and the background sounds can add authenticity. Radio journalists need to consider the ethics of adding noises that was not really there. Interviewing an airport manager about traffic delays in the studio and then adding archive sounds of plane cancellation announcements might not be representing the truth, even if it sounded 'better'.

Video

TV relies heavily on visual approaches to news and it will select stories for their visual appeal as much as for any other reason on a news bulletin. That means you need to be imaginative in presenting a story visually if the news editor is to be persuaded to use the story. Talking heads and archive footage are last resorts and you should attempt to consider unusual and active takes. You should be careful in the editing process that the impression given is what you want. The ability to strip 'snapshots' in time after each other in an order chosen by you should not be abused; the chronology of a story is an important element of the truth.

4

Researching the story

Having found your story, you now need to find out if it is something worth writing about. No good story comes to a reporter fully formed. Only boring press releases seem to contain ready-made stories – and that's only by the definition of the person who wrote it. The ubiquitous press release, indeed all story tips, should be scrutinised carefully to ensure they are not trying to disguise a story as something else. You need to discover the angle of the person selling you the story. All stories need to be checked out and sourced from elsewhere, with additional views added if needed. In order to produce good copy, reporters need to be able to trace a story back to its source. In practice, it is usually easier to have the sources and then work the story up from them. For this reason, a reporter is highly reliant on the sources that he or she cultivates. The wider the sources, the more you'll know – and the more you know, the better the stories.

The important thing to remember about any source, official or unofficial, is that they are telling you it because they want to. This might simply be because it's their job, or they're interested to talk to a reporter or because there's no real reason why they shouldn't; but whatever the reason, we are using up their time and their goodwill and they don't have to do it. Of course there may well be more complex reasons for them telling you things. They may have their own purpose in exposing the story they are offering you: they may want revenge on someone, to get them into trouble or expose them. They may want to win public support for a campaign. Nor can you rely on people telling you the truth, or certainly not the whole truth. Not that many people tell outright lies, in my experience, but of course they do bend the truth because they only hear part of an argument or only see what they want to see. You should always check with another source to verify information – until then, it is only a claim.

PEOPLE

When you first start work on a regional newspaper or radio station or move to a new area, you will need to contact all the organisations that are the source of most stories. This means getting to know press offices for all the big local companies and public authorities – local government, police, other emergency services, the local courts, health authorities and hospitals. Many of these will already have solid links with your paper or radio station but it is important that they develop a personal link with you. These formal sources are often a starting point for stories and most of these people will be happy to talk to you as they need you to publicise their pet projects and promote their own agendas, just as you need them to write stories about their pet projects and agendas.

Your local MP is an important source and will give you a direct access to what is happening in parliament. If your MP belongs to the governing party then you are going to get support for the government and its line. This can also give you some access to government ministers who are more likely to be invited in to talk about appropriate issues. An opposition MP is more likely to be on the attack though, and might be a better source of stories as he or she tries to build his or her profile. The PPC (prospective parliamentary candidate) is another good source as he or she will be trying to build a profile as the candidate who can win the next election, snatching the seat from the incumbent. In a marginal seat, which may have only recently switched sides, the pressure is likely to be high and both the MP and the PPC will be going all out to get a high media profile to help their electoral chances.

Local councillors and council candidates also need to keep their media profile high to ensure election or re-election. Teachers, vicars, shop-keepers, publicans and activists in local voluntary organisations are all funds of local knowledge and should not only appear in your contacts book but should be talked to regularly to keep you in touch with the local community.

There may be one or two celebrities in your area. Whilst these tend to be thickest on the ground in big cities or places with strong showbiz links such as Blackpool or Brighton, even the remotest place can have a celebrity, as the *Mull of Kintyre Gazette* found when Paul McCartney moved in to make the home of several thousand sheep world famous. Usually these celebrities are hoping for a bit of peace and quiet in their home area and you certainly can't use stories about them every day, but they should be cultivated so that the occasional low-key feature on their plans can help your readers feel they are on speaking terms with the stars.

Press officers

All government departments, local councils and moderately-sized companies these days have press officers. There is now sufficient media about to make it a full-time job explaining the council's or government's policy and presenting it in a positive light. Councils and the government have long since seen the need to employ people whose particular skill is to present their employer well to the media. This is a mixed blessing to the journalist. It is certainly useful to have someone whose sole job is to tell you things, but it can be annoying that a part of their job can also be to try *not* to tell you things, or worse still, disguise them as something else. At the end of the day, they are just people with a bit of news savvy, intent on presenting information about their employer in a good light – exactly the same as anyone else, but better at it and therefore more of a match for the journalist. Journalists can and should use press officers to their advantage, however. A good PR knows who to speak to in the company or council. They know how to get the information you need quickly and accurately. Don't be afraid to use them in this research role. They can often do a lot of the basic legwork for you. It is important to remember that the press officer will always follow the employer's policy line and so you will also need to build links elsewhere in the organisation. The press officer is useful for finding out basic facts and figures, but you may need to talk to someone else to find out what those facts and figures mean and how they may have been twisted or misrepresented. As always – never believe anything you are told until you've either verified it or worked out the person's motive for telling you.

Spin doctors

Spin doctors are often spoken about with awe or loathing. They are a variant of press officer so closely linked to the centre of power that they become part of it. This means they can be particularly useful to the journalist in that they can give a unique insight into what is going on – once you get past their very careful interpretation of the facts. Spin doctors often try to pressure reporters by offering unique titbits of information in return for 'favours' at another time. A reporter who has built up a strong relationship with a spin doctor may not want to jeopardise receipt of those titbits in order to print a damaging story from another source that the spin doctor assures them is completely untrue or is at least misrepresenting the facts. It is for this reason that the relationship can be difficult. One of Britain's best-known spin doctors must be Alistair Campbell, Tony Blair's spokesman. Like Sir Bernard Ingham, Margaret Thatcher's spokesman, before him, Campbell is an important Downing Street player who runs the PM's press office. His job is to ensure that his boss gets a good press and he does it well. There is a divide between the role of the press office in providing information about the activities of government and Campbell's role, which is more political and is about presenting Tony Blair and the Labour Party.

Experts

Experts can be called upon to add authority to a news item or feature. They are particularly useful for radio, which likes calling in local experts to add an authoritative view to a major issue of the day. Lecturers at the local college or university are OK. Top local businessmen, trade union leaders and local politicians are also standard fare. The key to a good expert is someone who clearly knows his or her subject, has an appropriate title and is able to give you a snappy, to-the-point quote quickly and easily. These people are hard to find and are worth keeping in your contacts book. Being able to get an authoritative quote on any subject from astrology to zoology quickly and without fuss is very useful. Radio and TV need to ensure that such experts look and sound the part. Interviewing a farmer with an Oxford accent dressed in a three-piece suit may not carry the same conviction as one in working clothes with a soft country accent.

Ordinary people

Although journalists need to talk to the powerful, rich and famous, it is often the ordinary person who is the really useful contact. The famous will probably contact your organisation if they have a story to tell, whether you are there or not. Equally they won't tell you anything if they don't want to, so they don't require cultivating in the way ordinary contacts do. Ordinary people get to hear a good deal of what's going on in their field, but won't necessarily tell you about it unless they know you well or you ask them.

'Ordinary' people include: committee members of local organisations and charities, trade union officials, teachers, health workers, lawyers, planning officers, police officers – the list is long because you never know who you are going to need as a contact. That's why it's so important for a reporter to socialise with as many people as possible. The official spokesperson will never tell you what they want to keep secret. The same principle applies in any organisation. The boss won't tell you anything, but if you talk to the secretary, or the person on reception, you may learn a good deal – not necessarily detailed information, but certainly an idea of trends.

If you are being kept waiting by the boss before an important interview – don't huff and puff about the damage to your pride. Charm the PA or secretary and try to find out as much as you can. Look to see who comes in and out and ask about them. This needs to be done with subtlety, although it is impossible to be so subtle that the person will be unaware they are being quizzed. However, done properly, it can appear to be merely idle interest and therefore of little significance. Chatting to a caretaker, secretary or sales assistant can often give interesting results. They don't always know all the details but neither have they been considered important enough to have been instructed not to talk to strangers and they can often see no harm in doing so. They can get to know a surprising amount about what's going on – after all, they do work there – and can certainly tell you things about the business or organisation you'll never hear from the boss. Everyone you meet should be cultivated because you never know when they'll ring you up with a story, or at least an idea for a story, or when a story will throw up someone you've met as the ideal contact.

Because of this, it is important to keep a note of who you know. Partly so you don't look a complete fool when they ring up and you can't remember them, and partly so you can contact them if you need to. Often this sort of contact starts you on a good story by talking about a rumour they have heard. Maybe your friendly local gasman tells you (after the third pint at your local) that's he's had to turn off the gas supply at a well-known local restaurant – probably because they haven't paid the bill. It is but a small amount of work the next day to find out when the restaurant is due to close because of their debts. A TV programme I saw contained a story about a local restaurant whose water supply had been cut off, yet went on trading – to huge health risks. Where was the local reporter with a contact in the water company?

REFERENCE BOOKS AND ARCHIVES

Although computers tend to be the first research thought of most young reporters, don't forget that there are a number of traditional reference routes that are still quick and easy. The phonebook is the easiest way of getting a local contact's address and phone number, while *Who's Who* does the same for the famous, *Crockford's* for the religious and *Debrett's* for the titled. There are numerous other reference books covering all the subjects one can imagine. Your own news organisation's library and archive can also be an extremely useful resource.

CONTACTS BOOK

Although your office will have a long list of potential contacts filed in an index system on the newsdesk, your own contact book is one of your most important possessions. Your sources are the most important resource you have. If you can afford it, a digital personal assistant such as a Palm Pilot or Psion Organiser is ideal. If you can only afford, or choose to have, paper, the best book to get is a small loose-leaf folder of the Filofax type. These are neat and convenient to keep up to date. A neat book encourages you to keep this vital resource in an easily-usable condition. Loose-leaf folders also allow you to add other data to the book if you want so that it becomes a complete resource.

If you can't afford this then any smallish notebook, preferably indexed, will do, provided it is easy to fit into a pocket or handbag so that you *always* have it with you. You never know when you will meet someone whose phone number you want, or when you will want to refer to it.

Entries in your book should be made with care so that it is easy to find the name again when you need it and so you know what the name refers to when you see it again. Don't be afraid to put the name in your book two or three times under different categories.

For instance, if you were to meet Joe Bloggs at a presentation ceremony at your local workingman's club you would obviously list him under Joe Bloggs. But you might also list him under Downtown Workingmen's Club (social secretary) and, after finding out that he was a railway worker and a member of the local NUR committee, you might well list him under your 'Rail' entry (possibly one or two pages long) as railway station worker (NUR committee). The recent spate of rail horror stories shows how useful it could be to have a contact on the inside of the rail system.

It is worth photocopying or duplicating your contacts book data on a regular basis. If it is a digital organiser then back it up on your desktop computer at least weekly. You could also keep your contacts on a computer address book, just printing out at regular intervals into your Filofax. It would be a disaster if, after two or three years of contact building, you were to lose your contact book.

Your contact book is your property and should not normally be shared. Never leave your contact book with anyone and never let the newsdesk or other reporters see or read it. It is, of course, up to you whether you share the information contained in the book, but showing anyone some of the names could lead to your sources being compromised. You have a duty to your contact. It is you they know and are prepared to talk to and they may be unhappy at being passed around the office as some sort of convenience. If you are willing to share the contact with a colleague, it may be appropriate to seek permission from the contact first.

When you enter a new name in your contact book, you should ensure you spell the name correctly, in full, so that you know your contact entry is correct and it can be used as a reference. It is imperative that you have a home and a work number (or any other number) so that you can contact the person at any time. An address is also very useful together with a note of their occupation.

If you are really efficient, then a date of birth and some personal details (jotted down after you have left the contact) can give you a major advantage next time you ring them, as it will appear you remember them, making them much more likely to chat. Don't overdo this, as too much information is difficult to keep up to date and can end up sounding creepy. Ringing someone you've spoken to a couple of times and asking how the kids are is one thing, but ringing them and asking, 'How did little Jeremy get on, because wasn't it his first day at school last week?' and 'Did Sarah pass that important dance exam?' is likely to get you locked up for stalking.

The Data Protection Act has some sway here and is another reason to be careful about passing on details. If someone gives you their name, address and phone number, it is reasonable to interpret that, for the purposes of the Act, as permission to store that information in order to contact them again in the future. But it should not be taken as permission to publish that name and address to colleagues, or in the paper, without specifically asking permission. Whilst at present the Data Protection Act only applies to material kept on a computer, within the next couple of years, it will apply to paper records as well.

COMPUTER-ASSISTED REPORTING

If you want to make something sound more effective, add the words 'computer assisted' in front of it! We've had computer-assisted design, computer-assisted diagnosis, and now we have computer-assisted journalism or reporting (CAJ or CAR). This is the latest buzz phrase from America and is, according to all the new media conferences in the UK, the coming thing.

There are three main types of CAR according to US writer Margaret De Fleur. The first is the collection of data and its manipulation from a range of on-line databases – most of them now part of the World Wide Web. The second is the setting up of databases to store data researched by ordinary means. This could include a straightforward list of contacts, but is likely to contain much more information, usually of facts surrounding a particular story. The third type of CAR is computer-aided investigative reporting that uses databases in the same way in order to investigate a story (De Fleur 1997: 73).

CAR (and CAIR) requires a stream of easily manipulated statistical data. In other words, the main use of CAR is the statistical analysis of data collected either from on-line databases or other sources in order to produce stories. An example I saw in a workshop I attended a few years ago included a database of hunting accidents in one of the US States. This database allowed the reporter to compare statistics for death and injury by place, time, age group, sex, type of injuries and so on. Anyone who has ever manipulated a database with a large number of fields (type of information held) and large number of records (the number of incidents) knows this can be loads of fun. You can quickly discover that more men aged 23–30 were shot in the arm on a Tuesday outside the town of Pope's Creek than anywhere else in the country. However, whilst this might be fun, it's not always news. As usual, all the computer-aided bit does is let you do something more easily and accurately that you used to do with paper and pencil. Just because you can manipulate data quickly to get stories doesn't always mean they will be more interesting.

An example of CAR used by Margaret De Fleur concerns an early use of the technique in the US when computers were still in their infancy. The director of a local government agency providing cheap mortgages for low income families was fraudulently giving cheap mortgages to influential citizens. The evidence of this was openly contained in the records, but since searching the paper records would have been an enormous task, it seemed unlikely anyone would ever attempt it. Reporter Elliott Jaspin managed to get the electronic version of the records and ran it through the paper's computers, quickly exposing the fraud (ibid.: 2). The point at issue here is that Elliott Jaspin and his fellow American reporters were able to demand the public records in electronic form. In another example, reporters on the *Seattle Times* were able to build a database of information on the Green River murders by getting hold of arrest logs, police expense vouchers, budget requests, internal memos, mileage logs and case reports. This helped them produce stories about the police's inability to find the killer (ibid.: 81). Even now we have a Freedom of Information Act in the UK, it does not offer access to the range of material cited above. Most of it is specifically defined by the Data Protection Act as sensitive personal data and therefore not information to be released without the data subject's consent.

Since the UK does not have as good an access to statistical data as reporters do in the US, there is less use for CAR. Some UK government statistics are now available on the web for loading into databases, but we are well behind the US.

USING THE INTERNET

However, just because we may be behind in our use of CAR doesn't mean we can't use computers to help us report. The Internet, particularly the World Wide Web, is fast becoming the sensible starting point for any research.

Whether you are finding out about a person, a place, a company, organisation, campaign, idea or leisure activity, there is likely to be loads of information on the web. Indeed, the major problem these days is not finding out information, but in narrowing down the amount you will get to a torrent you can cope with.

E-mail

E-mail can be an excellent way to get information from people who might otherwise be hard to contact. It is perfectly possible to guess e-mail addresses in order to be able to contact people who might otherwise be heavily screened. It isn't guaranteed, but it is surprising how often you can get an e-mail to someone to either ask a question or ask them to ring you. It is, of course, perfectly possible to interview by e-mail.

Most people's e-mail addresses are a mix of their name and employer address. The employer address will almost certainly be the web address, so to contact someone in the BBC, for instance, you might only need to type in a variant of their name and the BBC address. Since you can send an e-mail to several people at once, just work out all the name variants and make them a list. In other words, if you assume I worked at the BBC, just type into the address field of your e-mail sender: c.frost@bbc.co.uk, chris.frost@bbc.co.uk, c.p.frost@bbc.co.uk, chris.p.frost@bbc.co.uk, chris.frost1@bbc.co.uk. The address which ends with the figure '1' is because some e-mail addressers add numbers in order to differentiate between the same name. Hotmail does this for instance. It is entirely possible that you or a friend might have a Hotmail address similar to: Joebloggs78@hotmail.com. Obviously only one of these will reach your destination and the others will be returned to you. This will allow you to note which one (if any) worked. Keep the message general so that you can check if it is the right person without revealing sensitive information should the address turn out to be the wrong person.

It is also possible to search for e-mail addresses on several web sites, although I have yet to find these to be of much use since most rely on the person registering their address with the site. Many web sites will also allow you access to a search database for their staff e-mail addresses. Go to the University of Central Lancashire site, for instance, and you should be able to find my e-mail address.

Travels on the World Wide Web

The web needs to be handled with care in terms of the information that it gives. Because all web sites look reasonably professional, due to the software used and the way computers present information, even the maddest ideas and people can seem reasonably sane. In the good old days, spotting those with a seriously flawed bee in their bonnet was easy because they wrote to you on lined paper torn out of an old reporter's notebook (I always had the vague worry that it *was* an old reporter's notebook – some odd people work in newspaper offices). The writing nearly always seemed to be in green ink and would be heavily underlined or in capitals. Now the lined paper is a sophisticated computer graphic and the subtle green type is neatly presented in Times New Roman, like everyone else's, because your browser goes some way to determining how a web site looks on your computer and the web site's design ideas only seriously effect the way it looks if it is produced using expensive computer graphics. Since many reporters trying to search a number of sites fast turn off the computer graphics (something you can choose to do on your browser) even these are not always visible.

As with all material that comes into a newspaper office, web sites should be treated with a good deal of cynicism. Gradually you will get to know those sites you trust and those you don't; but any new site should be treated as merely the views of that author – whoever has produced it, the material will have been edited in some form.

Sites vary from the visually unexciting but extremely useful UK parliament site (www.parliament.uk) to the sometimes entertaining but virtually useless personal home pages. The parliament.uk site offers lists of MP's names and addresses. It gives the full text of Hansard, and the full text of all Bills and Acts of Parliament since 1997. Anything you want to know about what is happening in both houses of parliament is there and it is a great place to collect basic information about parliamentary politics. This site is about as close to an objective site as I can imagine. For a bit more subjectivity, but still looking at government, try the Central Office of Information (www.coi.gov.uk). This carries all the ministerial press releases, ministerial speeches and information from the various government departments. For even more subjectivity, still in the field of politics, try the various political party sites. These give details of leading politicians, their line on various policies and, of course, suitable attacks on the opposition. A quick look through these half-dozen sites can give you good solid background on the issues facing the UK political establishment and the various party viewpoints. You can become an instant political correspondent. There is a list of useful sites attached to the bibliography at the end of this book.

Finding names, numbers and addresses

The first thing you may need to know is the name of a person, whether they are the managing director of a company or a local politician. Getting names is usually easy – just ring the company or organisation and ask the switchboard. The web site can also help here and logging onto the company's web site will often allow you to find out who is in charge of what.

The obvious starting point to track down someone's phone number is the phone book or directory inquiries, but again the web can now be incredibly useful. Some company or organisation sites allow you to search for staff names and will offer you phone numbers and e-mail addresses. BT now has all phone directories in a searchable database on the web. Log in and type in the name and location of the person you are seeking. It will give all the alternatives.

The web can also be extremely useful for finding names and phone numbers in far away places. Want to know who's who in some far away town? Find the town's web site (they nearly always have one) and contact a local official or semi-official body. Perhaps the site lists the government offices or the local newspaper, a local tourist information office is even better. A quick phone call or e-mail to these sites can often get you local contacts. Often a local site lists important numbers like the local hospital or police force. It can be worth seeing if the person has a personal web site or is listed on another page. Type their name into a search engine and see what you get.

Newsgroups

Newsgroups are another good way to find contacts for a story. There are hundreds of newsgroups and you can subscribe to as many as you want. Your browser should allow you to choose newsgroups and you can add new ones all the time. Choose the subject you are researching and you will find all sorts of people from experts to beginners talking about subjects of their choice, whether that's UFOs, crop circles, air disasters, trains or their favourite pop band. You can then either join in or quickly identify someone who will be worth speaking to either by e-mail or by phone.

Chat rooms

Chat rooms allow people of similar interests to get together and chat. Mainly these are used as dating systems, or at least a chance to meet people, and so are of limited value to the reporter, but it is important to remember they are there and can occasionally be used as a way of contacting people.

Finding a site

Search engines try to make sense out of the chaos of the Internet. The Internet links together networks of computers which are themselves a collection of computers often containing thousands of pages of information posted by hundreds of users. This makes for millions of sites run by millions of users and it is impossible for the average human to cope with tracking down all that information. Since the number of computers being added to the Internet and the amount of information they can access is growing exponentially, this information overload is not going to go away.

Your main access will probably be the World Wide Web, which is actually only a part (although now by far the biggest part) of the Internet. Newsgroups and FTP sites make up most of the rest of the Internet, but you are unlikely to use anything but the web unless you are working in a particularly specialist field.

Direct searching

A direct search is where you type the domain name of a site you want direct into your browser's 'Address' dialogue box.

A domain address is made up of several parts. The first part (HTTP://) is the protocol and tells the computer how to read the file. There's no need to type in the HTTP:// part of the address these days; the main browsers add that automatically. The next part of the domain name is the individual address and the final part tells you something about the address, whether it is a company or an organisation, for instance, and the country of origin.

It is much easier these days to do a direct search for a site you want than it used to be because major corporations and organisations realise the importance of a good domain name. There are also more Internet Service Providers and companies are more likely to use their own server. This means web names are not as long and complex as they often used to be, although some can still be a little odd. When you are doing a direct search things can still be difficult, though. Would you find Marks and Spencer under MandS, M&S, Marksand-Spencer, Marks&Spencer, Marks_and_Spencer or some other variant of the famous retail giant's name? Are they perhaps part of a bigger holding company with its own name and web site? You also need to decide whether it will be .co.uk or .com. Since Marks and Spencer is a corporation, it will be one or the other, or even both.

There are a wide variety of domain extensions:

com – commercial
org – organisations, charities, campaign groups, etc.
edu – Educational
gov – Government
net – Internet-oriented material
mil – US Defence Department

If the domain name chooses to be country-oriented, then it will add a two-letter country extension on the end:

uk – United Kingdom
fr – France
se – Sweden
fi – Finland
jp – Japan
au – Australia

And so on. There are also different links for country-oriented sites:

gov – government
ac – academic
org – organisations, charities, campaign groups, etc.
co – commercial

Most big companies try to buy up all associated commercial domain options and link them all into the same site, so it is usually worth trying one or two of the obvious options. However, some companies who got into the World Wide Web a little late have found that many of the domain names they would like have been bought up. Dotcom names are at a real premium because they give international access. According to BT, all three-letter Dotcom names are now registered, no matter what the combination of letter. Many site names have been registered by quick-thinking entrepreneurs hoping to be able to sell suitable names to corporations at a later date. Some are on offer for sale on the web for up to $4m. It costs practically nothing to register and maintain a domain name, but it is well-known that getting the right name can aid searching. A domain name such as www.insurance.com could be worth a fortune to an insurance company and it can be no surprise to find that Fidelity Investment owns the site. This makes good names valuable. In order to keep track of what is out there in those millions of sites on the World Wide Web, we require directories, search systems and bookmarks.

Bookmarking

This is a basic system that you can run yourself to keep track of interesting sites that you have come across and use regularly. It is important that you keep your bookmarks as up to date as possible and that you go to some lengths to file them neatly and name them properly. Your browser will allow you to bookmark sites as you load them onto the browser. Your bookmarks, or Favourites as Explorer calls them, are kept in a bookmarks file, and it is worth taking a copy of this file from time to time to ensure you don't accidentally erase it. It would be a shame to have built up a record of good sites over several years only to lose it because your hard disk crashed.

It is also possible to edit the bookmarks into folders so that your list becomes manageable. You could have several thousand sites marked and it would be impossible to navigate this without some form of system. You can put folders in your bookmarks file so that, for instance, you can keep all the 'politics' sites together and away from all the 'journalism' sites. What folders you use are up to you, but they should help you to easily work out which folder a particular bookmark will be in. You can also rename web sites in your bookmarks to make it easier for you to remember what they are or how you use them.

Search engines

Search engines allow you to look for sites about a particular subject. They allow you to type in a word, or words, and then they go off and find as many sites as they can containing that word. There are now hundreds of search engines on the web and there are even search engines that only find other search engines. Some search engines have robots that continually search the Internet finding pages and sorting them and listing their entries. These cover a large number of sites but are often not well indexed. Other sites use humans to look at sites and decide how to index them and whether they are worth listing. Very few search engines cover more than 10 per cent of the web, which is growing too fast for most to keep track of. Some search sites now charge a fee for those who want to be listed. This pays for the engine to review the site and decide whether to include it. The $199 fee does not guarantee inclusion, only a review. Theses search engines hope to cover only the best of sites, therefore attracting people to use their search capabilities. It is clear already that the main existing search engines are having difficulty keeping up with both checking on all the new sites and deleting sites they have already listed but are no longer in operation. Choosing a site from a search engine listing only to find the site is no longer there is now a regular occurrence.

Some of the main search engines to try (in no particular order) are:

- Excite
- Altavista
- Yahoo
- Google
- Netscape
- MSN
- Hotbot

- Lycos

- AskJeeves.

AskJeeves is the odd one out in that this is a search engine that you can ask questions rather than type in words to be found. With all the other engines, you type in words that you would like to find sites containing. With AskJeeves you ask a real question, not that you always get a more sensible answer.

For instance if you wanted to find out who first used the phrase 'Journalism is the first draft of history' then on most search engines you would type into the search dialogue panel 'First draft of history'. This would get the search engine to trawl through thousands of web pages seeking that phrase and it would probably come up with hundreds of potential web sites, although none might tell you who wrote the phrase. Most sites would merely be using that phrase to their own ends. With AskJeeves you could type 'Who first said "journalism is the first draft of history"?'. It might not be able to find out either, but would give a different range of journalism-oriented sites that might have the answer. www.Searchenginewatch.com is a good site to visit to find out more about search engines and how to search them well.

Most search engines use Boolean algebraic rules to control how you filter all the web sites it has to offer. You need to imagine that each search engine is a gateway to a sea of web pages. You could put up a filter which would tell the engine to show you only those containing the word 'journalism' and the search engine will index a list of all the hundreds of sites containing that word. If you ask the engine to find sites with the words 'journalism' and 'computer', you will only get sites with both words in.

Algebra is used in slightly different ways by many of the sites but the basic rules are listed in the following table (page 39).

After searching for pages, you will often find that whilst you do not get a page that gives you what you want, you do get some idea of the terminology and language of that particular subject area and this can help refine your search. Try using the jargon of your research subject to find other web pages.

Directories

Directories are lists of sites divided into categories provided by many search engines. These can often be easier to use than a long list of several thousand web pages. Netscape, Yahoo, Lycos, Google and others all give directories. Type in 'business' and it will offer you a long list of sub-directories. Keep choosing sub-directories until you get to the web sites of your choice. These

Table 4.1 Using search engines on the Internet

What to type into search address	Finds and lists the following:
A word, e.g. Journalism	Any web page with the word 'journalism' in it.
Several words, e.g. Journalism, computers	Any web page with the word 'computer' or 'journalism' or both.
Several words added together, e.g. Journalism+computers	Any web page with the words 'journalism' and 'computer' contained somewhere in the page.
A phrase in quotation marks, e.g. 'Computer journalism'	Any web page with the phrase 'computer journalism' but not pages with the words 'computer' and 'journalism' separated by other words.
Several words added together with some excluded, e.g. computer+journalism-internet	Any web page with the words 'computer' and 'journalism' but not any that contain the word 'internet'.
Several words preceded by the word *title* (t in yahoo), e.g. title: Computer journalism	Any web page with the words 'Computer journalism' in the title.
A domain name preceded by *domain:* e.g. domain: Marksandspencer.co.uk	Any web pages from that site.
A host name preceded by *host:* e.g. host: uk	Any web page from the UK.
Combine any of above: e.g. computer+journalism+host: UK-'Computer journalism'	Any web page from a UK host that contains 'computer' and 'journalism' but not 'Computer journalism'.
Wild cards. This is an asterisk that replaces text, e.g. journal*	Any web page with words 'journalist', 'journalism', 'journalistic', 'journals', 'journalese', 'journalistieke', 'journaliste', etc.

directories rely on the people who register the web sites with the search engine placing the web pages in appropriate directories, something the search engines ask the site masters to do on registration.

Portal sites

These are sites maintained by special interest groups that carry some of their own information, but make a virtue out of carrying a large number of hyperlinks to other sites. Several journalism portal sites exist and a good example is

Journalism UK at www.octopod.demon.co.uk/journ_UK.htm. This site has little direct information and is just a list of journalism sites usefully categorised. Most UK newspapers and broadcast organisations are listed, as are schools of journalism, journalism organisations such as the National Union of Journalists and regulatory watchdogs such as the Press Complaints Commission and the Broadcasting Standards Commission. These are good sites to list as they are easy jumping-off points for other sites.

FIGURES AS FACTS

Statistics and figures are a vital part of the reporter's job these days, whether in the form of a balance sheet or a sheaf of statistics. Many reporters seem to take pride in saying, 'Oh, I'm no good at maths' as though it were a lifestyle choice, such as being vegetarian or wearing a beard. Obviously if they were a talented mathematician they would be working as an accountant or a mathematician or a statistician. They are working as a reporter because their skills lie elsewhere. But just as we would expect a statistician or accountant to be able to pull together a readable report about their statistics or balance sheets and might sneer if they couldn't, so it is reasonable to expect an intelligent reporter to be able to understand and read a basic balance sheet and understand the basics of statistics.

So much of the reporter's work these days is based around opinion polls, government statistics, balance sheets of big companies and council budgets that not being able to sniff out when you are being fed a line means that a reporter is virtually useless. Politicians in particular will feed you figures that they say show one thing when even a rudimentary glance shows that they mean something completely different.

Like all sources, figures need to be treated with caution and the motive for issuing them questioned. Why is this source giving me these figures? What do they hope to gain? Often this will tip you off to where the weakness, if there is one, lies.

But there are also some straightforward ways of fiddling with figures that can give a completely misleading effect. Say someone approached you with a poll showing that boys at a local public school had an average £10 a week pocket money compared with children at a local state school who averaged only £3.92? First I would want to know why the public school figure is a nice round number and then I would want to know the number in the survey. If it turned out that only six pupils at the public school were prepared to answer, and one of those received £30 a week whilst the other five received amounts varying between £3 and £5 while the state school surveyed sixty students with amounts varying from £1.50 to £7 then the whole survey would be pointless.

Remove the one child with £30 from the survey and you then find that the averages at the two schools are remarkably similar. It shows up one of the difficulties of averages.

Averages

An average is the first tool a politician, statistician or spin doctor grabs when they want to lie to a reporter without the reporter being able to accuse them of anything. We can easily say that the average citizen of Anytown smokes 2.4 cigarettes a day. Of course most Anytowners don't smoke at all, but those who do, certainly smoke enough, so that if you divide the total number of cigarettes smoked in a day by the number of citizens, you get an average in the region of 2.4. Once you learn that only 18 per cent of Anytowners smoke, but that they average 25 cigarettes a day, then you might feel you were getting somewhere, but even here there can be wild discrepancies. Smokers could smoke anything from one to 100 cigarettes a day. There might be quite a few who smoke between one and five cigarettes a day; a fair number smoking between five and twenty; a reasonable number smoking twenty to forty, but the numbers smoking more than that are likely to fall off rapidly. So these *arithmetic* averages (a *mean*) do more to confuse than to assist, and tells us little about the smoking habits of Anytown. We could have calculated the *median*, the point at which half the sample smoke more and half the sample smoke less, but this would be very close to zero, because of the high number of non-smokers. The *mode* gives similar problems as it measures the most frequently met statistic. According to this, Anytown is a non-smoking town. The problem with this example is the distribution of the data. If we learnt that the height of the average man in Anytown was 5'11", we would not need to know what kind of average it was as they would all be very close to each other. All adult males in Anytown will be between five and seven foot, with the majority being close to six foot. The data distribution graph would be shaped like a bell with a few people in the low five foot, a few approaching seven foot and the majority between five foot nine inches and six foot three inches. The mode, mean and median would be similar enough to differ by only decimal places. But in our smoking example, this isn't the case. The majority of people don't smoke at all, and then the distribution of smokers is very different to the bell shape of man's height. Many smokers only smoke a few cigarettes and only a few smoke more than twenty to thirty. The only useful statistics are that 82 per cent of the citizens of Anytown are non-smokers and, of the smokers, the median (the highest point on the distribution curve, the number of cigarettes smoked by more people than any other) is fifteen cigarettes a day.

Surveys

Lots of information is presented to journalists from surveys, whether produced by the government or private companies. The journalist's first concern needs to be about how the survey was produced: who was used for the sample, how many of them were there and how representative was it?

Most government surveys use large samples; often the total number of people available so their samples and the way they are selected can usually be trusted. If their sample says 75 per cent of those on benefit have more than three children it is probably an accurate figure because they have asked everybody on benefit (it is probably one of the standard questions asked on the form needed to request benefit). Only if people have lied about the number of their children is there likely to be inaccuracy. With governments, it is changes in the way things are counted year on year that are likely to throw up problems. For instance, a government might change the way it defines unemployment in order to change year-on-year comparisons.

In the private sector though, if a PR company sends you a survey claiming that 75 per cent of women found that a particular brand of wrinkle cream reduced signs of ageing after three weeks of use, then some serious questions need to be asked (such as, 'What are you doing even thinking about using such obvious advertising material?'). First you need to know how many women were sampled. If you were to find that it was ten, then the survey probably doesn't prove very much, particularly if it turned out that they all worked for the PR company. You should also start wondering how they got the figure of 75 per cent (75 per cent of ten people is 7.5).

You would also need to know the questions asked. If the question is, 'Do you think you look younger after using the cream?' then a 'yes' answer might be significant. But if the question was, 'Do you think you look older?', then it means that 25 per cent believed it actually made them look older.

At the end of the day, if you get a small enough sample, the random action of chance can appear to be statistically significant. For instance: I've just tossed a coin twenty-one times but only got heads seven times, or 33 per cent of the time, rather than the 50 per cent I would expect. Should I use the coin to try to win my fortune? No. What I haven't told you is that tosses 21 to 28 turned up heads every time. I just ignored the last seven throws and based my survey on the first twenty-one attempts.

Sample sizes are terribly important in surveys. Darrell Huff gives the example of a polio vaccination trial that vaccinated 450 children and left 680 unvaccinated. None of them later caught polio in the subsequent epidemic because the normal expectation was that only two of a sample this size would have been infected in any case. A sample twenty to thirty times larger would be required to give meaning to the trial (Huff 1954: 41).

Graphics, including graphs and charts, also need to be handled with care. Don't use any graph sent to you by an outside organisation; it has always been designed to present the information in the best light to suit that person or organisation's case. Get the graph redrawn by your art department using different criteria if you want to use a graph at all.

Percentages

One statistical tool that often confuses reporters and readers is the use of percentages. It is usually advisable to adjust percentages into fractions both for yourself and for the reader. A press release suggesting that more than half of the people sampled preferred the client's brand of breakfast cereal whilst only 49 per cent preferred their rival's cereal loses its punch when you rightly suggest that half prefer one and half prefer the other. Rounding the figures of 50.54% and 49.46% to half is perfectly legitimate, particularly if we find that the sample is fewer than the total number of customers of both cereals – as it is bound to be.

Percentages should always be thought of as ratios and not as fixed numbers. A 20 per cent increase of 120 is 24 to give a new figure of 144, but 80 per cent of 144 is only 115.2. Percentages are a good way of comparing one number to another but fractions usually do the job better and more clearly. To say a road is twice as busy rather than that there is a 100 per cent increase in traffic is much clearer because many people are confused about whether doubling means a 50 per cent, 100 per cent or 200 per cent increase.

Finance

I have an exercise that I like to give to student journalists which involves them looking at a balance sheet to try to find a story. Most of them find this an extremely difficult exercise and some even question whether it is right for them to do it, pointing out that they are not accountants.

Finance is an important part of everyday life these days and many stories in newspapers concern it, whether it is the budget of the local council, talk of the government's economic state, personal finance, private pension funds, the profit levels of major companies or whether a local firm is due to go bust, placing scores of local citizens out of work. Companies in the finance world are always keen to trumpet their successes, explaining when they are doing well, but are a bit less forthcoming when things go badly. The modern reporter needs to be able to understand finance and read a balance sheet. How is government spending our money? Are people being ripped off by insurance or pension giants? What are fat cat directors of privatised companies being paid? Is the biggest employer in town financially stable? All of these figures are available from press offices, on the Net, Companies House or market analysts. The point is can you find the story from the deliberately confusing figures?

Essentially all companies and organisations must issue accounts. For local government, this is done annually and the accounts are audited before release. Audit is a legal process that involves auditors checking the work of the accounts department that drew up the accounts to ensure that the accounts are accurate and that no fraudulent practices have been used. In reality of course, it would be impossible for any audit firm to go through the accounts of a large organisation like a county council and check that every receipt matches every payment actually made to the supplier, that the payments were fair and that the goods or services they represent were used in full by the council. Nor can they check that every entry in the council's accounts is accurate. However, by using the techniques of their trade, they are able to certify that there appears to be no faults with the accounts and that all money spent was used legally and honestly. Private companies also have their accounts audited annually.

Accounts are produced in two main sections: assets and liabilities, and income and expenditure. These must balance so that if there is more income than expenditure (a profit) there is a commensurate increase in assets or reduction in liabilities. If, of course, there were more expenditure then there would be an increase in liabilities. This allows us to very quickly look at the asset/liability position and see whether the company is worth more or less than it was a year ago. A healthy company should be worth more, certainly not less, but just because a company's liabilities increased substantially in any particular year, does not mean that it is in trouble. Perhaps the company has paid out a lot in a streamlining exercise. It has closed down a loss-making plant and this involved large costs in redundancy payments and demolishing the old plant. They would have borrowed money for this that would increase the company's liabilities. But now, expenditure would decrease substantially since money would not be poured needlessly into that plant and the company's expenditure for the following year would be substantially reduced, even taking into account the loan repayments. Profits should rise and the company's assets would increase. It would also be able to pay a bigger dividend to shareholders.

Private companies are usually owned by their directors. These are normally the people who started the company or their descendants. Bloggs and Sons may not still be owned by Bloggs nor by his sons (or daughters) but it may well remain in the control of the Bloggs family. Eventually, if Bloggs and Sons continues to prosper, the company will want to expand and will require more money than either the company or the individual Bloggs can provide. They might then sell shares in the company to other people. These could either be offered privately to people they know, or offered publicly to anyone who wants to buy them.

Maybe the company is worth £3m after being in business making Christmas decorations for fifty years. The grandson of the founder has just taken over as Managing Director and has negotiated an enormous order for decorations with a massive retail company in Germany. It will triple the company's turnover, but they do not have the capacity to make the decorations in their present factory. They need £2m urgently to build a new factory. The bank is not prepared to lend so much, but a local Lottery winner is looking for some-where to safely invest some of his winnings that will give a good return, but that will be reasonably secure. If he were to invest £2m in a bank, he would receive interest payments (at 2000 rates) of maybe as much as 5 per cent per annum. The original *capital* sum would be safe and he could withdraw the £2m having made up to £100,000 per year. But by buying shares in the Christ-mas decoration company, investing the much-needed £2m, he could find that the company does well and pays him a *dividend* worth 6 per cent of the face value of the shares at the end of the first year. The new Managing Director proves his worth and the company continues expanding. Not only does the shareholder continue to get a substantial dividend (£120,000 per year) but the value of the shares increases and after five years, the Lottery winner finds that not only has he been receiving a total dividend of £600,000 but his shares are now worth £4m on the open market. Of course, the shareholder would have to pay tax on the income and tax on the capital gain. Since the rates for income and capital gains will be different, this would affect any decision about where and how the investor would invest. Of course, as they say, the value of shares can go up or down. So while the bank was a safe bet, as you can remove the full value of your capital at any time, a shareholder could lose money if the company fares badly as many who rushed to fund the new Dotcom com-panies found to their cost.

PROFESSIONAL PRACTICE

There are a number of ethical issues the good reporter needs to bear in mind while contacting and dealing with sources.

All the regulatory bodies take this very seriously and agree that journalists should treat contacts fairly. The BBC has pages of excellent advice to offer its journalists about how to behave ethically while researching a story in its Producers Guidelines (www.bbc.co.uk/info/editorial/prodgl/index.shtml).

Often friends and relatives of a criminal or the victim of a disaster or accident are some of the first people journalists approach to follow up a story. These people are often unwilling to take the public stage, have done nothing personally to justify it and are doing so during a time of considerable emotional difficulty. The BBC warns: 'Although full reporting of the facts surrounding notorious criminals may properly entail reporting of their family circumstances, we should always try not to cause unnecessary distress to the innocent' (www.bbc.co.uk/info/edtl/prodgl 2000).

Victims of rape or sexual assault, and victims under the age of 18, are protected from being identified by the law. Naming them is an offence under several different Acts of Parliament. But even victims who are not directly identified should be treated with care. Journalists need to ensure that they do not join the criminal in damaging the victim.

There are, of course, other ways of gathering information that are unsavoury or unacceptable. Stealing the rubbish of a subject in order to get an idea of their lifestyle is borderline criminal and certainly unsavoury, although it is done by some journalists and private detectives. The police, of course, routinely inspect rubbish while investigating a crime because it does sometimes prove to be a useful source of information. Benjy the Binman is well known on Fleet Street for making a living going through the rubbish of the famous – or infamous – and selling the results to newspapers.

Often a newspaper will be offered papers that point to a superb story but have been stolen. Taped recordings of phone calls or bugged conversations fall into the same category. Only undeniable public interest could justify using (or gathering) such material.

Sometimes a paper or magazine will pay a source for access to a story. Whilst paying Posh Spice and David Beckham a huge sum to have exclusive access to cover their wedding is little more than an extension of their life as entertainers, paying witnesses for the evidence they will give in court can risk prejudicing that evidence. The Press Complaints Commission (PCC) has introduced a clause into its code to consider this:

> Payments or offers of payment for stories, pictures and information, shall not be made directly or through agents to witnesses or potential witnesses in current criminal proceedings or to people engaged in crime or to their associates – which includes family, friends, neighbours and colleagues – except where the material concerned ought to be published in the public interest and the payment is necessary for this to be done.
>
> (PCC 2000)

The BBC normally forbids paying witnesses before a trial. There are one or two exceptions: overwhelming public interest or because the interviewee is an expert witness whose professional opinion is being sought.

Bribes, corruption and conflicts of interest

In my experience, bribes are not very common in the British media in the terms of a plain envelope stuffed with fivers, but threats, pressure and hidden bribes in terms of freebies are. You should always be on your guard when free trips, parties or other gifts are mentioned. The NUJ code of conduct says:

> A journalist shall not accept bribes nor shall he/she allow other inducements to influence the performance of his/her professional duties.
>
> (NUJ 2000)

5
Office procedures

Any journalist hoping to find stories and publish them for a particular reader-ship has to be up to date with the news because otherwise it is impossible to identify what is news. So it is important to read newspapers, watch TV, listen to the radio and scan web sites. It is also important to keep up to date with all the gossip within the community on which you are reporting. If you are working for a local paper, you need to know what local people are saying and who is who. If you are working as a parliamentary correspondent, you need to know all the MPs and the gossip about them. You may not use this informa-tion for stories, but you do need it for background, if only to ensure you are not publishing stories that are weeks or even months old, which will damage your reputation for providing up to the minute news.

THE NEWSROOM STRUCTURE

All newspapers or broadcast stations have a newsroom where reporters work. Some larger newsrooms may also contain other editorial staff such as sub-editors, features staff, library, sport or photographers. These are usually the main newsrooms for a paper or broadcast station. District offices are usually just reporters possibly led by a district news editor. Many radio stations and newspapers have district offices. The BBC has many small district radio studios usually with one reporter. This will have a sound desk and an ISDN (digital telephone) link to the main studio so that the reporter can report live or send packages. It can also be set up so that people can come into the studio to be interviewed from the main office.

All newspapers and broadcast stations are structured in much the same way. The editor is in overall charge of the editorial operation, but day-to-day man-agement of the newsroom is in the hands of the news editor. This may be an assistant editor (news), a news content manager, or on a small paper it may even be the editor – but whatever the title, their role will be to supervise reporters, ensure the stories they want covered are covered and ensure the editor is kept in touch with what's going on.

They may also commission *freelances*, organise *stringers* and liaise with sub-editors, photographers, advertising and other departments in the organisation. In a big office, the news editor may have several deputies and assistants. This is particularly true of a daily paper or a radio or TV station where the news operation is six or seven days a week. Even news editors need time off.

A big newsroom may have some reporters working as correspondents, specialising in some aspect of news work: education, local government, crime or health, for instance. Some may have correspondents for aspects of work that are particularly important locally. Maybe it is a rural area and a farming correspondent is needed, or a seaside resort requires a tourism correspondent. There would then be a pool of general reporters covering the everyday work. A chief reporter is sometimes appointed. He or she might help run the diary,

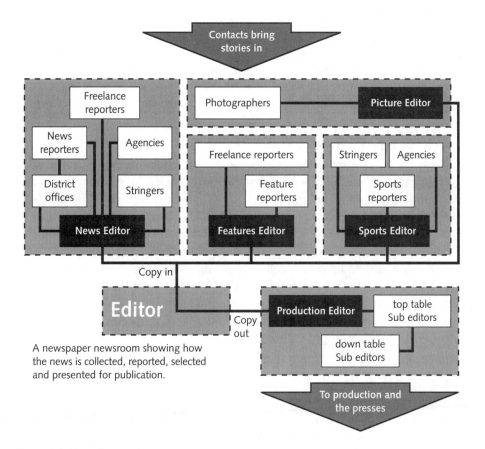

A newspaper newsroom showing how the news is collected, reported, selected and presented for publication.

Figure 5.1 Copy flow in the newsroom

or it might be a courtesy title for a well-respected reporter taken off diary to work on his or her own initiative. In addition, stories are often produced by freelances and stringers.

Freelances are self-employed journalists who often prefer working for themselves as it allows them to pick and choose the work they do. This can suit those with a specialist interest or who want to work part-time to fit in with family commitments. For instance, it may be that a local freelance specialises in finance and normally sends copy to the financial papers. He or she may only send copy to the local paper if a story of local interest is found.

Stringers are local people who write a few hundred words every week about their community, social group or sports club. These are usually rewritten by sub-editors, but occasionally contain a good story that requires extra work from a reporter. A local journalist can also work as a stringer for a national.

THE NEWS CONFERENCE

Just as you need to keep up to date, so does the news editor so that he or she can make decisions about the news. The news editor will also notify photographers if pictures are needed and will keep the editor and the chief sub-editor in touch with the progress of the more important stories. It is vital that you keep your news editor in touch with what's happening: the key issues that are likely to bubble up and affect the future of a story.

The news editor needs to know what stories are available and when they will be ready for publication. These stories will then be discussed by news conference; a gathering of all the editorial executives. On a daily paper or local radio station, there will be at least one conference a day and possibly more. A conference early in the day will discuss the latest news to go on the live news pages for that issue of the paper or the next bulletin. It may then go on to discuss the overnight pages, early pages for the next issue of the paper. A later conference will then update the situation. The conference gives all the executives a chance to detail the stories or pictures they have for the next paper and explain how they envisage using them. This gives the executives a chance to liaise so that the editorial team produces the best product possible.

THE NEWS BRIEFING

When a news editor asks you to do a story, he or she should provide you with a briefing about the story and its potential, together with any paperwork to support the story – council minutes, a report or a press release. There may, of course, be no briefing at all apart from, 'Get to such and such by this time and see what's going on'. Make sure you understand what it is the news editor is after. He or she should tell you the kind of story hoped for, how much space (or time) may be available and where it's likely to go in the paper or bulletin. Instructions such as: 'I'm looking for this to lead an inside page', or 'I'm looking for twenty to thirty seconds from this', should give you some idea of what's expected. This does not mean you need to stick rigidly to the brief. If the circumstances have changed radically when you arrive, plans may need to be rethought. You should alert the newsdesk so that they can reconsider what they want to do. It's no good dashing back into the office two minutes before deadline to tell the news editor that everything's changed and the story's now worth the front page or five minutes at the top of the bulletin. It may well be too late to make those changes. But if you warn the news editor as soon as you can (mobile phones make that easy these days) then he or she can have made arrangements to change the running order so that things are all ready if you come back with the goods. On radio, the reporter should also brief the news editor on the type of treatment the story is getting, such as a live two-way discussion between the reporter and the presenter, an interview or a package.

If you are working on a story of your own, tell the news editor about the story and its strength in a memo, phone call or chat, depending on the urgency of the story. If you are out and about and see a news event such as a major house fire, then a phone call is clearly the way to contact the news editor, so that he or she can arrange coverage. Remember – don't just ignore the job you had been going to unless the news editor says so.

OFFICE DIARIES

The office diary is kept by the newsdesk and contains all the notes on news-worthy events in the area along with a note of who is to cover them. The news editor will mark up the diary every day based on events notified to him or her through the post, over the phone or from editorial staff. Many of the events will be notified by press release. The news editor will put the item in the diary and store the press release in some sort of filing system alongside it. He/she will then append a set of initials alongside the event to show which reporter has been chosen to cover it.

All reporters should check the diary at least twice a day. Once in the morning, after the news editor has checked the post and once in the evening before going home to see if there are any new evening jobs or early calls. Checking more often is a good idea.

If your initials are alongside an event, check the time and the date and then see if there is a press release or some other notes in the filing system. If there is, check this against the diary entry to ensure the diary entry is correct and then copy the details into your notebook and leave the notes in the file. Then everyone will still know where they are should anything go wrong.

On-diary/off-diary working

Working to the instruction of the newsdesk, covering stories in the diary is called on-diary working. This is the staple of most newspapers and all new reporters start here. But as you become more experienced, the news editor may give you more opportunities to work on your own initiative. This is called off-diary working and is much more exciting either because you have initiated the story or it is a fast-breaking news drama. The best way to persuade the newsdesk to let you work on your own initiative is to show the news editor you've got some. Start bringing in stories of your own. Then you can start asking the news editor to let you have time to follow up ideas that you've had. You'll need to brief the news editor on the idea, so be sure you know enough about the story to give him or her some idea of what it's about and what you hope to get out of it in copy terms. The story doesn't have to be the next Watergate, but it does need to be something you've managed to find out about from personal contacts. A good time to approach the news editor about this kind of story is when things are quiet. If the diary is already crammed and the newsdesk is rapidly running out of reporters, it is unlikely you will be let loose on your pet project. But if things are quiet the news editor may well be prepared to give you a chance. Once you've proved that you can come back with good stories found and developed yourself, you are more likely to be allowed to do it again.

STORY SUPPORT MATERIAL

Press releases, reports or minutes are often provided to help you write a story. Whilst these can be a great help in producing the story, it is unwise to rely on them too heavily. Names can be misspelt or facts used incorrectly. As always, you need to check. The same is true of your own organisation's archive or library. Just because you've carried a story before, does not mean the facts in it are right and you should be very careful about using old cuttings or library records.

The Press Complaints Commission carried a warning in its March 1992 bulletin: 'Cuttings are an essential part of newspaper research but too many journalists now seem to act in the belief that to copy from 10 old stories is better than to write a new one with confirmation by proper fresh enquiry' (PCC Report no. 7 1992: 2). The PCC went on to give two examples: one, a newspaper strung together information from several newspapers to produce what they presented as a first-person interview. In the second example, a magazine put together a number of reports and invented dialogue in the magazine's style to produce 'an article which contained serious inaccuracies and was to a degree fictitious' (PCC Report no. 7 1992: 2).

Embargoes

Press releases often carry embargoes. These say that the story can only be used after a certain date or time. A good example of an embargo comes from the Central Office of Information when they send out details of the New Year's Honours list. This is embargoed until midnight on December 31 so that the secrecy of who is getting what award is not breached. However, they realise that it would be impossible for any news organisation to then get in touch with the people on the list in order to interview and photograph them so the list is sent to newsdesks earlier so they can arrange for interviews and pictures. This means that the newspaper can have pages all set up for distributing from midnight onwards and broadcast outlets can also produce bulletins from midnight on with archive footage, new pictures and interviews.

As embargoes can be useful to journalists, it is often in their interest to adhere to them. But they are not legally binding in any way and if misused, can be ignored.

Faced with an embargo, you should alert the newsdesk. If you think the embargo is unreasonable, then explain this to the newsdesk, but it will be up to the editor to decide.

Names and addresses

Publishing names addresses can also be problematic and there may be times when this is not appropriate.

Members of the police force or the armed forces, for instance, are often concerned about revenge or terrorist attacks and so it is regular practice for the police and armed services to refuse to name serving officers. Publishing their names is usually not the problem, but publishing addresses could put them at risk and so most media limit an address to a town.

The PCC published guidance about addresses in its August 1992 report. It advises regional newspapers to publish only the street name and not to identify a particular house by name or number partly to protect the news source and partly to reduce 'the possibility of error: if you do not publish the number, you cannot get it wrong' (PCC Report no. 12 1992: 5). This would be normal practice for broadcasters as well. While a national broadcast station would rarely give more than the town, even local broadcasters would not normally use the house name or number.

The PCC warns journalists not to encourage the harassment of individuals named in their stories by publishing telephone numbers or addresses:

It is true that in the case of prominent people addresses are readily available but the press is not under an obligation to make it easy for cranks and criminals by saving them the bother of researching telephone books and directories.

(PCC Report no. 12 1992: 5)

The PCC upheld a complaint against a newspaper which, after giving the address of a prominent individual's weekend home in Wales, suggested: 'He had better not tell the Welsh nationalists or they will come and burn it down' (PCC Report no. 12 1992: 5).

You should also be careful with addresses in stories that make it clear the house is likely to be empty for a period. Many a newly-married couple or recently-bereaved person has returned home to find they've been burgled because the newspaper published their address.

Groups of people you should be particularly careful of publishing addresses for are:

- police officers;
- prison officers;
- members of the armed forces;
- people (especially women) whom the story indicates are living alone;
- children;
- celebrities;
- judges;
- magistrates;
- those accused of very serious crimes;
- the relatives of those accused of very serious crimes;
- AIDS victims and their care workers;
- domestic violence and abuse shelters;
- Lottery and other prize winners. The Press Complaints Commission issued specific guidance in PCC Report no. 29 (1995: 32).

Journalists should be particularly careful to refrain from publishing the addresses of refuges and shelters for those who have been the victims of domestic violence and abuse. This would put the people seeking refuge and the workers in the refuges in danger. 'The very purpose of the refuges is invalidated if addresses are made public' (Frost 2000: 87).

6
On the road

Although the phone and the Internet have become much more important as a way of contacting sources, many reporters still spend a lot of time on the road. This is particularly true of broadcast reporters, who still need to speak to people to get that all-important sound interview or video footage, but newspaper and magazine reporters still prefer to sit face-to-face with their interviewee whenever possible.

LOOKING GOOD

All reporters need to be neatly dressed and reasonably well-presented. You never know at the start of the day who you may be speaking to. You may wish to dress like a Goth in the evening, resplendent in black leather and silver buckles, but this is unlikely to help your interview with the local mayor. Your hair, make-up and possible body piercings also affect how people view you. Knapp and Hall point out that 'The length of a person's hair can drastically affect perceptions and human interaction' (1997: 223). One often hears people, especially teenagers and young adult, saying that the way they dress, wear their hair or adorn their bodies should not affect the way they are perceived. In an ideal world, of course, they might be right, but in such an ideal world, these youngsters would probably cease to wear such extreme fashion items to express individuality, peer identity and rebellion because such fashions would cease to be perceived badly by those in authority (Knapp and Hall 1997: 230). This all suggests that the way you look plays an important part in how you are received. If you want to rebel by looking like an extra from *Conan the Barbarian* you are probably better doing it at night with your friends.

Whilst at work for a mainstream news outfit you can't go wrong with a suit and a raincoat, which is why so many reporters wear them that they have become a stereotype. There is a risk that you end up looking like a cheap imitation of one of the leads from the *X-Files*, but then FBI agents probably dress this way for the same reasons. A suit or sober jacket and matching trousers are safest and you need a coat that protects you from the wind and rain on the doorstep, but that doesn't leave you baking when you are stuck with wearing it in a hot, stuffy magistrates court. (Your speed of exit in order to file the copy at the end of the case may not leave you time to pick up scattered belongings.) This mode of dress (as the X-Files prove) applies to both sexes. If you are working for TV, then that uniform is even more important. You are being pictured in thousands of people's homes. Better to look smart than scruffy. Hair can be more of a problem for men. One can get away with reasonably lengthy hair these days provided it is kept clean and tidy, but if you insist on it being long, even with a ponytail, it might adversely affect your ability to get a job. Type of hairstyle is less of a problem for women (unless you choose an extreme style or colour). It is important that TV reporters of both sexes have their hair styled regularly. Visible body piercings for either sex should probably be left out during work time, particularly for TV. Your interview with the Prime Minister is not likely to be taken as seriously if your eyebrows and nose are chained together.

If you are working for a specialist publication serving an audience where the dress code is specific, then it is possible to dress in that way. You will soon get to know your audience and the type of people you regularly interview and what they wear. Reporting for *Club Scene* or *Bass and Drum* magazines would allow a reporter to wear much more casual clothes than I've suggested above. But even here, it's probably better to be the best-dressed (or at least the coolest-dressed) person.

OUT AND ABOUT

It is vitally important that you keep in touch with the office. It's much easier these days, but even the best-behaved mobile can run out of battery or leave you in a communications black spot, so being able to use more traditional methods can still be important. Should your phone let you down, do ring the office and let them know and then ring in regularly so that they know what's happening. Always keep your eyes open for telephone boxes. Get yourself one of the credit-card style phone cards that give you a pin number and allow you to phone anywhere from anywhere, putting the cost of the call on your, or better still your employer's, phone bill. Failing that, one of the voucher type phone cards can be bought anywhere. The former is more flexible and will be provided by BT free of charge. The better newsrooms will allow you a card on their phone number, otherwise get one on yours and charge its use on your expenses. Either way, the card allows you to use phone boxes, sometimes even after the cashbox has been vandalised. You don't even need the card provided you can remember the number. You can even use them on private phones and assure the person that the cost will be billed to you.

If you end up in a job that requires long-distance travelling you must learn to find your way around strange towns. Seaside towns are always easy – just head for the seafront and everything will be close at hand. Inland towns can be more difficult. Aim for the railway station. This is often just off the centre of the town and is always signposted so it is easy to find. Short-term parking at the station is often fairly easy so that you can leap into the newsagent that will be on or near to the station and buy a street map. Rail staff are often good people to ask for directions as they know the locality and are used to people asking directions. The local rail station also often carries posters with information of local value and the bus station can be similarly useful. The town may be big enough to have a tourist information office or there may be a local council office that carries out the same function.

Alternatively, service stations carry a wide range of goods and it is always worth popping into the first one you see on arrival in a strange town to buy a street map. These usually cost only a pound or two and make finding that obscure address much easier. The person at the till may well know more details and may be willing to help once you've bought a map. If you get time of course, look the town up on the Internet before leaving home or the office. Some web sites carry quite detailed street maps of towns and cities.

Phone boxes are also useful because they have the location of the box printed on a card near the phone. If you get lost, they can be a simple, reliable way of finding where you are in the middle of the night. Of course stopping and asking a passing pedestrian or calling into a service station or shop can be even more effective. If you are after the address of a specific person, then you could try the electoral register. These are available in libraries and post offices. If you know approximately where the person lives then inquiries at the local post office, newsagent or perhaps the video shop may well find the address for you.

In the car

Your on the road experiences will tend to vary with the type of paper or broadcast station you are working for. A weekly or local radio station is unlikely to ask you to do more than hop in your car for the fifteen-minute trip to the outskirts of town. A national broadcast station or newspaper could have you living in your car for days on end. Whilst writing this, scores of reporters were covering a major foot and mouth outbreak and heavy snow falls in the north of England and Scotland, all in inaccessible countryside.

Most reporters find a car of some sort is a must and you need to keep it properly equipped – not just so that it is roadworthy, but also so that you waste the minimum amount of time on the way to a job. Always keep your car stocked with the following; you never know when you might be stuck in the middle of the countryside for days on end.

- A couple of bottles or cans of drink – if you are stuck on a job miles from anywhere, you might need it.

- A Mars bar or similar long-life foodstuff for the same reasons.

- A heavyweight anorak with a hood – it can get cold and wet out there! You also may need something to cover up or disguise your office clothes.

- Waterproof hat or umbrella – Keeping out the wet becomes a high priority after you've spent day after day in the rain. An umbrella is particularly useful for broadcast journalists who may need to do an interview in the rain.

- Wellington boots – trekking across fields or building sites make these essential.

- Phonebook and Yellow Pages – phone boxes never have these and you will need them. Always carry a copy of your local phone book and Yellow Pages if you work for a local paper or broadcast station. Getting phone numbers and contacts nationally is much easier these days with mobile networks and it is probably worth your while paying for one of the network subscriber services that will find numbers for you. Alternatively, using a WAP phone, you can access BT's Internet version of the national phone directory and this might be a lot more convenient. If you have a laptop, then it is possible to get a CD containing all the phone directories or containing every name and address in the country.

- Street maps – you can't know everywhere, so it is worth carrying street maps of all the major towns and cities in your area.

- Road atlas – see above! It is worth carrying a UK atlas and then one that is more detailed for the region you are in.

- Spare notebook, pens, batteries, tapes or digital disks – these are absolutely essential, especially for broadcasters. You can often buy a new notebook, pen or batteries at a local shop or garage.

- Mobile phone – you should always have this with you, but just double check before leaving on any job.

- Charger for your mobile phone – one of those that plugs into the cigarette lighter of a car as well as the mains version.

- Cash – keep a £10 or even a £20 note hidden somewhere safe in the car. It's amazing how often you have to dash to some God-forsaken village, only to find you have no cash to buy food and drink and there are no cash machines. At least this will let you buy something at the local shop. It's worth remembering that many shops and garages offer a cash back service, but this doesn't work with credit cards, so make sure you have a debit card with you as well.

- A phone card – for that frustrating moment when your phone runs out of battery and refuses to recharge.

- A battery-powered razor can keep male reporters looking presentable. Women reporters often find a spare pair of tights can come in handy.

Other transport

Journalists spend a fair bit of time on the road for their employer. Even working for a small weekly paper sees you out and about fairly often.

For those without car, local travel on public transport or taxi requires you to keep receipts of travel or tickets. Your company may well have an account with a taxi firm, in which case you'll be obliged to use them. If they insist you use public transport then keep timetables of buses or trains handy so you can find your way about.

Many companies insist you drive a car even in the centre of the biggest cities and will pay you a mileage allowance for its use. These will vary but should be in the high thirties or low forties per mile these days. You should keep a log of every journey you do; where you go, when and the return mileage so that you claim the full expenses at the end of the week. Don't forget to keep car parking receipts so that you can claim these.

Don't forget to let your insurance company know you are using the car for business. This might increase your premiums but non-disclosure could invalidate your policy. It is always worth shopping around insurance companies for the best policy. Some include cheap membership to one of the breakdown organisations, and this can be a useful saving.

Occasionally companies will have a company car or van they will expect you to use, particularly for radio where you may be expected to use a radio car equipped with all you need. Remember, it is your responsibility to ensure the vehicle is roadworthy and fully equipped with the bits and pieces you'll need. You are the one who will be prosecuted for any road offence such as bald tyres or faulty lights or be shouted at by the news editor if you run out of some vital technical requirement. The station cannot insist on you breaking the law by driving an unroadworthy or illegal vehicle.

Check the tyres, windscreen wipers and washers, brakes and lights. If they are not working, don't drive it. While you are at it, check the bodywork. Note any scratches or dents. You do not want to be held responsible for someone else's mishaps. Any serious damage to the bodywork could make the vehicle illegal to drive. Check on the insurance. Not only should it be up to date, but it should cover you completely. You do not want to become responsible for an excess on a company vehicle.

You would normally only use train travel for long distance journeys. Most companies limit their staff to second-class travel, but insist on first-class if you are to travel by sleeper. This will ensure you get a cabin to yourself. Second-class travel on sleepers in the UK could mean you sharing the cabin with a stranger. In some sleepers abroad, even first-class travel could mean you sharing a sleeper with up to three other passengers. If you have to buy your own ticket, always explain to the ticket seller where you want to go, when you want to return and any other special needs. This should ensure that you get the right ticket even with the complicated ticket packages in the UK. If you are abroad it should ensure that you will be sold the correct ticket and told of any local oddities. In many European countries, for instance, you need to validate the ticket in a date punch machine on the platform before boarding the train. Insist on a receipt at the station and keep this and your ticket safe so that you can claim it back. You should get into the habit of always storing receipts in the same pocket of your wallet or Filofax, so that you can find them no matter how drunk you were the night before!

Travelling abroad

Only the lucky few travel regularly by plane. Always book plane tickets through the company's agent in advance unless the job is a rush one. Scheduled flights can be heavily booked, especially just before weekends and public holidays. If you are in the kind of post that's likely to see you jetting off at a moment's notice, then it is worth trying to persuade the newsdesk to issue you with a company credit card to allow you to buy tickets rather than using your own card. Give the agent approximate travel times and don't be too fussy about which airline you use. This only becomes significant on really long haul flights.

Make sure you don't need a visa – plenty of countries will not allow you access without one. The Foreign and Commonwealth Office will give advice. Their web site is a wealth of useful information and has specific pages of advice on every country you are ever likely to travel to. Visit www.fco.gov.uk/travel where there is a country list you can choose from. It will give you details of visa needs, trouble spots and local customs. You don't need a visa to travel in EU countries, but some of the former East European countries might require one. America requires you to apply for an 'I' visa if you are working as a journalist to media at home. If you are working for US-based media then you need a different visa. Many countries requiring a visa will sell you one on arrival in the country (e.g. Turkey). Many require you to get the visa first, but can arrange it on the same day from their embassy or consulate. For instance, you can get a visa to travel to India on the same day from India House in London. Some visas take longer and you cannot travel until you get one. Get a visa for as long as possible, after all, you might have to go back.

Only intercontinental flights have first-class these days, so the choice is usually business class or economy. Most companies insist on you travelling economy. While this is acceptable for short-haul flights around Europe, I think it's asking a bit much to expect someone to leap straight into a difficult job at the end of a twelve-hour flight in economy – push for them to pay for business, there are a number of good deals about these days if they shop around. Business class means more space and much better seating, which can be reclined properly in order to get some sleep. It also means slightly better meals. The facility to use business lounges in airports is the major advantage. While the business lounge in European or American airports is a pleasurable improvement, in some developing countries' airports it's a necessity. You may have to wait hours before your flight and business lounges ensure access to working phones, fax machines, the Internet, and good-quality food and drink. Attempting to find this in some of the world's airports might be quaint, even amusing, while backpacking around the world, but it is an additional unwanted pressure if you've been working on a story for fourteen hours and are now trying to catch a plane overnight to another continent where the time difference means you've got to be in a press conference forty minutes after landing and filing copy an hour after that. Check-in and check-out is also easier when travelling business as there is usually an express facility that means you can leave it much later before arriving at the airport and still get through much quicker.

On European flights, though, business class merely means sitting in seats where the middle seat of the row is turned into a table. Since with a bit of planning you can often sit in a row of three seats with no one in the centre seat and still travel economy. Business class travel in Europe is grossly over-rated. The use of the business class lounge on transfer flights is not to be sneered at, but on straight non-transferring flights, there is little to be gained by travelling business class.

Always aim to sit in an aisle seat. Watching the view soon palls, whilst easy access to the loos, being able to flag down stewards for extra food or drink or move to a more congenial seat easily are major benefits. You will also be able to leave the aircraft quickly. If you travel light enough, then you should be able to get your luggage in the cabin with you. You can take a surprisingly big bag as hand luggage and I have often travelled with my small shoulder bag, laptop and a decent sized grip (large enough for a week or so away) inside the plane. They are likely to be even more lenient if you are travelling business class. In EC airports, you will rarely be asked to show your passport in detail. Just wave the cover and it's straight into customs and then out to the taxi ranks. Non-EC countries are more difficult but at least you'll be near the front of the queue for immigration.

All except the very shortest scheduled flights offer meals. The longer the flight, the more substantial they are so there is no need to get to the airport early in order to eat.

If you travel in this country or abroad fairly often, keep a bag permanently packed. Keep it in the boot if you travel to work by car. It should contain a wash bag with toothbrush, toothpaste, comb, shampoo, soap, deodorant, aspirin, salve, plasters, razor, antacid, any other medications you need; two changes of underwear, two tee-shirts (for warmth, nightwear or just for a clean change), night wear, coffee sachets, creamer sachets, power plug adapter, spare notebook and pen, can of drink, bottle of water, pack of biscuits, sewing kit, emery board, scissors, shoe cleaning kit and a paperback for those long waits. If you don't carry your driving licence and passport with you all the time, keep them in this bag. Move to a safe place on your person once you are on the move.

You should have a full passport and if you do not possess one, get one soon. Often the best trips and freebies are announced at short notice and require your passport. One reporter made his career because shortly after starting with a national paper he was the only reporter in the office with his passport on him the day a big story blew up. His news editor despatched him direct to the airport and he made the most of his opportunity.

If you can afford it, keep a £20 note (or more) in the bag or its equivalent in travellers cheques or US dollar bills. Hard currencies can usually be exchanged anywhere. It is getting easier to get by with just a credit card, but there are still places in the world where using one is difficult.

If there is any chance of you travelling to the Far East or Africa, then it is worth purchasing sterile hypodermic needles in case you happen to need medical treatment. The risk of AIDS from infected needles in these areas is very much higher than in Europe or America. Boots and other chemists sell medical packs for travellers that contain these sorts of supplies and it's worth investing in one if you travel a lot. It's also worth keeping your jabs up to date. This is partly so you can leave at short notice, and partly to ensure you don't have to have about ten at once in order to travel somewhere at a week's notice.

If you have this lot ready in a decent bag (heavy-duty woven nylon about 60 cm × 30 cm × 35 cm with hand grips and shoulder strap and at least two outside pockets) all you need is to pack as many days' worth of clean clothes as you need and you are ready for anything at a moment's notice.

Never pack more than six days' worth of clothes. Use laundries or buy cheap clothes abroad and leave them there. You don't want to be cluttered with loads of bags – you'll have enough to carry with important things such as your notebook and computer.

Men will find a jacket and trousers the best wear as this means packing just a few shirts, a couple of ties and a spare pair of trousers. Women will find that a jacket with matching skirt or trousers will serve a similar purpose. Women need to take care about clothing that covers the arms, legs and chest in some of the Islamic countries – it might be politically incorrect, but then it's their country.

Choose clothes that will combine well with each other and that are easy-care. It might mean you presenting a similar image all the time, but you will be able to cope easily with weather changes just by adding additional layers of clothing.

Airports are international communities and you have to travel a fair way to find one that won't accept sterling, but once you are outside, you are on your own. Always carry a minimum of £10–£20 worth of the currency of your destination (don't carry too much in case you are mugged and spread your credit cards about for the same reason). Remember to get local currency at the airport on the way through. If you have checked-in early enough, you should change money at the departure airport. Credit cards are useful for banking abroad. Paying for trains or taxis demands cash. Some taxi drivers might take dollars or sterling, but the exchange rate would be awful. Watch out for local customs. In India, for instance, it is wise to take the police-registered taxis. These cost slightly more (although still very cheap by Western standards) but the police take a note of who you are and where you are going when you leave the airport. This gives some protection against being driven off and attacked by the taxi driver or his friends.

Many airports are well served by train systems and these are often the fastest, and certainly the cheapest way to get into the nearest city. Ticket sellers at most train stations, certainly in Europe, nearly always speak serviceable English provided you are talking trains.

Unless you are travelling to a country where alcohol is illegal, it is often worth buying a bottle of duty free booze to take with you on the trip. Alcohol can be expensive in some countries and being able to offer drinks in your room could give you the edge over competitors. Women should be wary about who they invite to their room and a small hip flask in the handbag might be a better bet. Remember that alcohol is illegal in many Islamic countries and taking drink there would be a big mistake.

A place to lay your head

If you are staying away from home overnight, you will need a hotel room. Get your newsdesk secretary to book the hotel before you leave so that the billing arrangements are made direct to the company. This will ensure a reasonable hotel with the bill sent direct to the company. If they can't arrange to pay direct, make sure you know that. You don't want to end up paying twice.

Most hotels in Britain are now far better than they used to be. Any hotel with two stars or better will ensure a clean room with a comfortable bed, en suite bathroom, telephone, TV and coffee-making facilities. Usually there will be a bar in the hotel as well. Minibars always seem undersupplied and over-expensive to me. Either carry your own choice of alcohol or use the hotel's bar on a cash basis. One colleague of mine allowed his room to be used for a bar bill once and woke in the morning with a splitting headache to find two strangers sharing his room and a bar bill of £400.

A hotel with fax facilities and a photocopier could be useful, although it's not difficult to find an office bureau in most towns. Many service stations and local shops have photocopiers for hire these days. Don't pinch the towels at hotels but do take some of the soaps, shampoos and sachets of coffees to make up for the hotels that don't provide them.

Some private guest houses or one-star hotels can offer excellent accommodation, so if you are on a fixed claim rate, it can make sense to look at some of these. Check out the lobby and public rooms. Are they clean, and well maintained? If so, the rooms may well be. Ask to see a room before booking in. A reputable hotel will not object. If the room is up to scratch, leave your bags there and go down to check in. This ensures you get the room you've checked. Don't be fooled by apparent luxury. Check the bed, check the bathroom, check the view: are you overlooking a factory that will start work very noisily at 5 a.m.? Is the room next to the lift, noisily disgorging drunken conference guests at all hours of the night?

What may seem fine in the quiet of a pleasant Sunday afternoon will be entirely different at 5 a.m. on a cold, wet, busy Monday morning. A clean, private bathroom with plenty of hot water and towels is another essential. Don't forget, you may be living here for some days. Mobile phones have made the hotel phone less important these days, even if you are working abroad, but if you do use it, beware of running up big bills, especially if you have no credit card and limited cash. Do the kettle and TV work? Both are important if you are going to be stuck in the hotel room all evening. Satellite or cable TV can be important abroad as it will often give you an English language channel and a chance to keep an eye on what the competition is up to.

Check on the power points. You may have a laptop and you'll certainly have a mobile. Most power supplies for these are intelligent and will be able to deal with any difference in voltage. However, you will probably have to get an adapter for the plug. Check the instructions on the power supply before you use it. Some may require you to alter a control before plugging in to a different voltage supply. If all else fails, find a local electrical shop and buy a new power cord or charger suitable for the local power supply. When you check out of a hotel, you may want to stay in the town for some while before catching your plane. Ask the hotel if they'll look after your bags. Don't forget that many foreign countries still have left luggage lockers at airports or train stations. This will allow you to leave your luggage there for a few pounds while you carry on working.

PERSONAL SAFETY AND SECURITY

Your personal safety is important when you are out and about. The Suzy Lamplugh Trust sells leaflets with sound advice (www.suzylamplugh.org). Most of it is fairly obvious, but one of the surprises about obvious advice is how often people refuse to take it. Make sure you lock your car if you leave it and lock it anyway if you are inside it at night. Having remote central locking is a useful accessory should you need to make a snappy get away, particularly if you are sharing the car with a colleague. An attack alarm or a dog deterrent is invaluable at the right moment, although not if they are at the bottom of the glove compartment or a handbag. An attack alarm can be just enough to put off some would-be attacker who you've managed to upset, at least for long enough for you to get in the car and away. You need to ensure they have working batteries rather than carry the alarm about for six years only to find it doesn't work when you desperately need it.

Letting your office know where you are and ringing them before you go in to interview anyone is a wise precaution. You should always make sure you have plenty of fuel in your car and never let the tank go lower than quarter-full. Membership of one of the motoring breakdown services is also essential to ensure that should you break down, you'll be moving again as soon as possible.

It's worth checking whether your insurance company offers you a special deal. Several offer hefty discounts to RAC or AA membership as part of their comprehensive package.

Safety at home

Safety is usually a matter of common sense, but often a reporter's desire to get a great story can get him or her into trouble. Covering events like large-scale demonstrations that become riots can be dangerous and you should take care.

When covering potentially dangerous events you should choose your clothing carefully so that you don't look like a police officer or a rioter. Some reporters wear their press card on a chain or clipped to their clothing. This might help in some situations, but it could antagonise in others. It certainly might prevent casual conversations with people at the event that are often useful. You should avoid antagonising anyone. Arguing with a demonstrator could quickly attract a crowd who might turn ugly.

Avoid getting caught in the middle. Talk to people at the edge first so that you have enough material to do a basic story yet can slip away easily. Always keep your eye on an escape route to a safe area and ensure it remains clear. You should bear in mind any police instructions and ignore them only if you think you will be safe doing so.

You should always take care with expensive equipment. Just because the protesters are opposed to recreational drugs being illegal, won't prevent one or two of them permanently borrowing your tape recorder, camera or other equipment. Keep it hidden away where possible and certainly try not to be obvious with it.

If you are arrested, don't resist. The police might well use 'reasonable force' and worry about the potential bad press later. Try to get receipts for any equipment confiscated. Make sure you know the PIN number for your press card. All the press cards issued under the national press card scheme have a PIN number to allow the police to identify that you are holding the card legally. Show the card and give the PIN number when requested by a uniformed officer. If you are a member of the NUJ, there is an emergency number you can ring for immediate legal help and you should memorise that number or have it somewhere you can get it easily (in your mobile's memory for instance – but remember, that will be confiscated if you are arrested or may already have been stolen).

Safety abroad

Scores of journalists are killed each year around the world and many are hurt or arrested. Working abroad raises plenty of safety issues and if you are going anywhere off the beaten track or with a poor record for journalistic safety, try to get on one of the safety courses that are run these days for journalists, government officials and business people. They are not cheap, but they are better than being killed or ending up as the next terrorist kidnap victim. The International Federation of Journalists has an excellent little booklet with much advice and the Committee to Protect Journalists and Reporters Sans Frontières are among several organisations that also offer advice.

No story is worth getting killed for and if the situation gets dangerous, get out. Often it can be bureaucracy or obdurate officials that can be the problem. Always be polite and cooperate. The last thing you should be is obstructive. Remember, you may not have the same protections as you have at home. It is always easy to arrest journalists on trumped up spying charges and it may be days or weeks before you even get to see someone from your embassy. Be prepared for it all to take a long time, particularly if you don't understand the language. Keep asking for a phone call to a lawyer or the embassy but, above all, stay patient. The Foreign and Commonwealth Office offers advice on English-speaking lawyers abroad on its web site. It might be worth checking here before you travel. It's always worth learning enough of the local language to seek medical help, ask for food and water, get to see the person in charge and to ask for a telephone.

The IFJ advises that you should always carry your papers with you when you travel, along with plenty of cash – you may be able to buy your way out of trouble. Watch what you wear. If you are with a lot of military personnel, you might wish to be easy to differentiate. But if you are in a lonely part of the country, you might want to blend in. As one journalist pointed out: 'Earlier this year I was near the Afghan front line snapping teenage soldiers. Alan Pearce, the BBC correspondent, calmly suggested that the bright orange fleece I was wearing – Marks and Spencers, much admired – was not quite the right thing in the circumstances' (Jenny Matthews, quoted in the *Journalist*, January 1997). You might also want to consider a flak jacket if you are travelling in areas where snipers, mines or shelling are a risk.

The bottom line as always is to do your homework, think about the risks and plan for them where you can. One can never remove risk entirely, and life might be less exciting if one could, but you can minimise it to maximise your safety.

7
Making contact

People are nearly always the key to a good story – good witness statements or quotes that explain how the people involved feel about the issue adds to the strength of a story.

You need to plan carefully who you intend to speak to in order to get the facts of the story (the who, what, where and when) and who you need to interview in order to give it depth and drama (the why and the how). You need to interview a sufficient breadth of contacts to ensure that you are getting to the truth and not just a small part of it.

Take the example of a road accident. You might talk to the police and the other emergency services first. They will tell you in fairly professional and unemotive language what happened, as far as they know, and when and where it happened. This flat, dispassionate telling of the drama of a road accident in which people were injured or even killed is fine for official reports, but we really need to get at the human drama behind what has happened.

This can obviously be done in several ways. The first is to talk to people about those injured or killed in the crash. Perhaps there was something special about their life or even their death that makes them particularly interesting. Maybe one was a well-loved school teacher and her class of six year olds is to hold a special service in the next day's school assembly. Perhaps one victim was a local politician, national celebrity or a notorious criminal. The Princess of Wales's death, for instance, is just a small, boring road crash in Paris of no interest at all to UK readers until you add the extra ingredient of a royal celebrity passenger. Then it's a story worth millions of words.

There could be something special about the crash itself. This could be anything from the make of vehicles involved, to the site of the crash. An accident involving two steam rollers (and I mean a steam roller, not road roller) would be of more interest than two modern family saloons; an accident at a notorious blackspot already responsible for six deaths that year is also destined to be a bigger story. An accident caused by a driver having a heart attack or being momentarily blinded by a hooligan with a laser also adds a twist that makes the story more interesting. It is these extras that give stories what some editors call the 'pub factor' – that is, when a drinker in a pub turns to their companion and says, 'Did you see that story in . . . ?'.

So who do you speak to when you've found out the basic facts? If you are following up a story about a local hero or celebrity, you need to talk to family and friends. In the example of the teacher, you would talk to colleagues, friends and family. You would also talk (after getting permission from teachers or parents) to the children. Don't forget pictures. Is there one of the teacher with the school children? Can you get a photographer to the special service? Pictures of children clutching handkerchiefs or little posies of flowers say more about the reality of the relationship between the teacher and pupil than you possibly could, no matter how much space you were given to write it.

If the people involved were of no particular interest but the circumstances were, then you would need to talk to a different set of people. If it was mechanical failure then maybe you would need to talk to the garage that last serviced the car (they often put little stickers in the window of the car to remind the driver of the date of the next service – have a look and see if you can see anything like that). If it is a regular fault with that type of car, then talk to the press office of the car manufacturer. If the accident is caused on a blackspot then local politicians and action groups would probably be delighted to speak to you and then you can get an official comment from the local authority.

Never forget to talk to the 'little people'. It is often tempting to speak only to the police officer in charge of the situation or the politician complaining about the accident blackspot or somebody's press officer. But often the people who witnessed the accident, or are only peripherally involved, can give you an angle on the story that others can't. Theirs is a vital voice in telling the story whether as quotes in print or direct in a broadcast.

This is particularly true of stories that are not so cut and dried as a road accident. Talking to the managing director about whether his company is going bust will only give you the official line. Talking to the workers who are going to lose their jobs will give you a much clearer idea of the truth. It may not be material you can use but it will help you decide whether to continue with the story.

BUILDING TRUST

Of course talking to people requires you to be able to deal with people and quickly build their trust. Observations like, 'Things seem a bit quiet around here' dropped casually into the conversation are not easy to do unless the subject has already fallen easily into conversation with you. This can be difficult because you are not really in a position to introduce yourself as a reporter without them instantly refusing to talk to you. This means that you are attempting to get information by subterfuge, and that is unethical. However entering into a conversation doesn't seem to me to put a reporter badly into an ethical grey area, provided the reporter doesn't then use that conversation directly. This also doesn't stop the reporter from then introducing him or herself and asking more formal questions provided you realise that this will almost certainly dry up the information unless the person concerned holds a grudge or has some other motive.

No matter who we come into contact with we need to build a relationship. Whilst many people in official positions will give you the bare facts of a story, that's all you'll get. In order to add reaction or comment to that, or to expand on the basic facts, you will need to get them to warm to you a little so that they relax and allow their more human side to show. There are two ways you can do this: by your appearance and by your conduct. As soon as we open our mouths, we are judged. Instant assumptions are made about us by others. Assumptions about our intelligence, our background, class, race, education, abilities and, ultimately, our power. We have to give them a message that says, 'I'm interested in you. Talk to me. Trust me.'

Fight self-consciousness and show that you are confident and in control. Take charge of the situation – the subject will usually be happy to submit; after all, it's often a new experience for them and they will be happy to rely on you to guide them through it. While you are talking informally, listen carefully for any free information and be ready to respond. For example, if you ask how they are, they may tell you they have just returned from holiday in France. Do not let it pass without asking, 'Did you have a good time?' You need to be interested in the person for themselves and not just for what they can tell you. Body language is important if they are going to trust you. You need to stand close enough so that they feel you are interested, but not so close that they feel uncomfortable. Eye contact and smiling is vital. Do not fold your arms or put your hand up to your mouth. These are 'stay away' signals! If they are an important contact, offer to meet them for a drink after work. Politicians and police officers have particular pubs or clubs where they go to relax with their friends. If you meet them socially, you are likely to meet other people, who may turn out to be valuable contacts in the future.

CULTURAL EXPECTATIONS AND PROBLEMS

Reporters are used to dealing with people from all sorts of different backgrounds, but for many people, dealing with strangers is a new and difficult experience. Psychologists suggest that when we meet someone new from our own culture we are usually guided by norms and rules of behaviour that allow us to predict or explain their behaviour (Gudykunst 1994: 18). But when we meet someone from a different culture, these guides may not apply. Since from a psychologist's viewpoint, a different culture could mean someone from a different class, background, gender or race – never mind from a different national culture or religious background – this applies to many people we meet.

In addition, journalists often meet people who are under a particular stress or pressure, even if it is only the knowledge that their words will be printed for all to see in the newspaper and this can lead them to behave in a way that is unusual even for them.

Gudykunst says there are two main elements of uncertainty that people try to reduce on meeting a stranger. The first is when we are unable or unsure about predicting how the stranger will behave (ibid.: 19). The anxiety often felt by people on being accosted by a drunk in the street is this type of uncertainty. The normal rules of behaviour are not being applied by the drunk and we are unable to predict how the drunk will behave. This makes most people feel uncomfortable and they will break off the contact as soon as possible and leave. The second type of uncertainty arises when we are not able to explain a stranger's behaviour.

One of the major problems a journalist often faces on first contact interview is described by Habermas as *pseudocommunication* (Henley and Kramarae 1991: 34). This happens when people who

> share a common language and many common experiences, are likely to mistakenly assume that a consensus exists among them concerning the meaning of communicative behaviours. This mistaken assumption 'produces a system of reciprocal misunderstandings which are not recognised as such' or pseudocommunication.
> (Cahill 1998: 77; quoting Habermas 1970, Henley and Kramarae 1991: 34)

If someone assumes, for instance, because of the reporter's polite inquiry about their activities, that the reporter is actively sympathetic, they may say more than they would normally intend, working on the assumption that the reporter will protect them from themselves because of the reporter's sympathetic approach. When this later turns out to have been a mistake, the interviewee can often blame the reporter for betraying the trust that was only ever a one-way thing. This sort of behaviour can usually be detected by the reporter in the closeness of the responses and also in the use of language that indicates the interviewee's belief in a common bond. This might include specialist language or contacts named or gossiped about as though they were common friends. Whether the reporter wants to use these indications as a sign that he or she should attempt to put some distance between them by cooling down the contact and risk persuading the source to shut up all together, or whether the reporter risks being later accused of betraying the contact's trust, is a decision that can only be taken on a case-by-case basis.

When reporters set up a relationship with a contact, they are trying to find out a lot about them very quickly. Reporters need to break down the usual social barriers to find out details of intimacy the contact would never normally share with a stranger. In major incidents this is often not a problem. Psychologists tell us that people talk much more freely when disaster threatens, hoping to gain information and to pass it on (Shibutani 1966).

However, when the story is a normal, everyday occurrence, we have to work harder at building a relationship with the person. For this to be a real relationship on the contact's part – which is what the reporter wants – there has to be warmth and trust. This puts the contact in a very vulnerable position. The reporter learns a lot about them because of this position of trust. This artificial relation building is often seen as highly cynical and is certainly part of the reason why reporters are often portrayed as cynical, shallow and manipulative. However it need not be so. Just because the relationship has been manufactured for a specific purpose, and there may be little expectation of continuing it, does not mean that reporters have to completely betray that person. They are hoping for a fair and accurate account of their side of the story and it should be within the reporter's gift to give them that. If there is a feeling of betrayal and the reporter has done his or her best to be fair and accurate then it should be relatively easy to use that relationship to explain.

According to Argyle, all cultures have greeting rituals but these can vary widely (1988: 62). Whilst working in your home country, these rituals will be well known to you and should be followed, but if you are working abroad, try to adapt to the local rituals and, if you are meeting people from abroad, please try to be considerate to their rituals. This will make you less alien and ease the process of relation building.

Once conversations are under way, try to be aware of what is cultural difference and what is just the person's personality. Argyle identifies six elements of potential cultural difference, listed overleaf.

- *Proximity, touch and gaze* vary extensively. Britons often feel uncomfortable talking to those of Arab descent because they stand closer than the British are used to whilst talking.

- *Expressiveness* varies from race to race, from the so-called inscrutable Japanese to highly expressive Africans.

- *Gestures* and the use of certain words can also vary with a gesture or word being acceptable in some cultures, but not others.

- *Accompaniments of speech.* These are the responses we give when being spoken to and are cultural. Argyle tells us that 'black Americans often annoy white interviewers or supervisors by their apparent lack of response while listening' (Argyle 1988: 69).

- *Symbolic self-presentation.* Whilst some badges and symbols can seem obscure, their meaning can be very important. I visited China in the 1970s, and all soldiers were supposed to wear the same uniforms so that rank was not detectable. But, in fact, it was easy to tell the officers by the number of pens they carried in their breast pocket. Designer labels are our society's modern equivalent.

- *Rituals.* Argyle warns that it is easy to cause offence by ignoring the rules of local etiquette. 'Pike (1967) reports the case of a missionary who got into difficulties with a cannibal chief because she tried to throw him to the floor (shake hands) and laughed at him (smiled)' (ibid.: 69).

There may be a limit to how far you need to go in adhering to local customs and rituals. Whilst a white, Western woman reporter might be well advised to wear concealing clothing when reporting from Muslim countries, she would have to ignore many of the customs with regards to women in order to get the job done.

Just as there can be difficulties in the initial meeting, so the conversation or actions of a stranger can be misinterpreted, particularly if that stranger is from a different background. 'When we are communicating with strangers and base our interpretations on our symbolic systems, ineffective communication often occurs' (Gudykunst 1994: 27). Gudykunst goes on to point out that we often don't realise these misinterpretations have actually happened. There are several reasons for such a misinterpretation, including the obvious unfamiliarity of language on at least one side, but it is also possible that one participant does not have the cultural background to understand what the other means (ibid.). Once, when in India, my host was in awe of a public building he was showing me. It was an important building, but not particularly imposing. I finally realised that he was incredibly impressed by the wood panelling throughout the building, something I discovered was rare in India. Wood, I was told, was rarely used because it was very expensive, but it might also have been that its upkeep in the hot, damp climate of India would also have been difficult and expensive. Yet coming from a country where wood is often used to decorate even relatively modest buildings, I had not appreciated its full significance.

Gudykunst gives another example of misinterpretation with the example of a white, middle-class teacher in the US interacting with an African–American student raised in a lower-class subculture. 'The teacher asks the student a question. In answering the question, the student does not look the teacher in the eye' (Gudykunst 1994: 27). He goes on to describe how the teacher would in all probability interpret this as being disrespectful or showing that the student was hiding something because that is the behavioural norm in middle-class, white America. For a lower-class African–American however, lowering the eyes would be seen as a mark of respect. This misunderstanding could lead to ineffective communication.

As well as problems with different national cultures, journalists need to be aware that the differences in indigenous culture can be as great. There are huge differences in approach to conversation between different classes, races and genders in the UK. Henley and Kramarae identify a number of different theories of male/female miscommunication (1991: 20) saying the two most influential are: 'Female Deficit' theory, which 'identifies it [women's language] as inferior to "neutral" or men's language and as contributing to women's inferior status' (ibid.: 21), and the 'Two Cultures' theory, which suggests that 'Men and women come from different sociolinguistic sub-cultures, which have different conceptions of friendly conversation, different rules for engaging in it and different rules for interpreting it' (ibid.: 24). Whatever the cause, both male and female reporters, need to be aware of the difference in approach and interpretation that may be needed when talking to someone of the opposite sex or from a different sub-culture.

Several areas are identified by psychologists as being the most likely for miscommunication.

Minimal response or PMR. The minimal response (the uh-huhs or mm-hmm of conversation) are important for the reporter as they are an encouragement to the interviewee to continue telling the story. But we rely on them in all conversations and Maltz and Borker say that the positive minimal response is used by women only to confirm that the speaker can still hold the floor and that the listener is listening. Men use it to confirm support for what is being said. These differences help explain why women often complain that men aren't listening and why men complain women are always changing their mind. Women saying something of which men disapprove will not get the

PMRs they require while men take the PMR to express approval when that is not what the woman meant (Henley and Kramarae 1991: 25). Phrases like 'Oh, I see' are more neutral and can ensure that is the most likely message taken from your PMR.

The use of questions is another area of difference. Women use them to maintain conversation while men use them to request information. This means that a reporter using questions is more likely to get strict answers from a man but might get more of a conversation from a woman, particularly if the interviewer is a woman. Interviewers of both sexes need to be aware that disguising questions when talking to men might get more of a conversation going, which might get broader and more interesting responses.

The use of names can also tell us a lot about the reporter's approach to the contact. Whether the reporter uses Mr Jones or Bill can say a lot about the class and relative position of the interviewer and interviewee. It is wise to always use the full surname and title with strangers unless invited to do otherwise. The risk is that otherwise some subjects will be dominated by calling them by their forename. 'Now tell me, Mary, how did it happen?' reduces the status of the elderly person, shop assistant or home carer to whom it was addressed in a way that 'Now tell me, Mrs Jones . . .' does not. The only probable exception is children under sixteen years of age. It sounds impossibly formal to address a twelve-year-old as Master Smith – better to use a forename.

ETHICS

There are a number of ethical issues journalists need to consider when dealing with people. A reporter's dealings with children (or those who are chronologically adults, but are not in any other sense of the word) need to be carried out with the permission of responsible adults and usually with an adult present. This could be a teacher or a parent, but might be a medical worker or some other agent. Even with adults, reporters need to consider carefully the questions they are going to ask and the effect this will have on interviewees.

Intrusion into grief

The PCC, BBC Producer's Guidelines and the NUJ Code of Conduct all warn against intruding into people's lives while they are grieving. The death of someone close affects us all in slightly different ways and the reporter should be particularly sensitive when dealing with people in this situation.

The *death knock*, as it is known, is a situation that few reporters relish. There has to be considerable public interest in a story before a reporter should approach a grieving relative. Having said that, relatives are often very keen to talk about their loved one. As a society, we find handling death difficult and consequently tend to ignore people who often want to talk through their loss. They have lost someone close, often suddenly, under tragic circumstances, and want to talk about them. They want to explain to the world what a wonderful person their loved one was, why it is such a disaster that the person died and why they miss them so much. These can be difficult interviews. People talk in clichés, because they are too distraught to think in any other way. The reporter must also be much quieter than normal, allowing people to say what they want in their own way. It is an interview that may take much more time than normal – you can't rush away when you have what you want. Disengagement can take time and tact. You should never do such an interview by phone or e-mail.

Often newsdesks will ask you to get photographs. Always ask permission to borrow photographs and ensure they are returned. Remember that official school photographs may well be copyright of the photographer, so make sure you take some home-produced snaps in case there is a problem later. You won't want to go back again.

Door-stepping and harassment

Often when journalists are pursuing major stories, they need to *doorstep* people who are deeply involved in a story but refuse to speak to the media. This can be particularly difficult if many reporters (a press pack) besiege the person's home or work place. Even someone who is willing to talk can feel intimidated by a pack of fifty or sixty reporters, photographers and film crews all yelling questions and setting off flash guns. More reprehensible examples cited by Presswise, a charity dedicated to supporting the victims of such incidents, have seen scores of reporters walking around a person's garden, looking through windows, yelling through letterboxes and keeping the phone ringing off the hook while the person they are seeking cowers upstairs, scared to even come down. This can be a difficult problem to deal with from both sides. The press want to speak to this person and the person has the right to refuse.

These days, the police often act as facilitator. The local force press office may arrange a press conference for the person at the centre of attention. Or they may interview and photograph the person themselves, providing a transcript and pictures to the media. While this is bound to raise accusations of the police attempting to control the media, it can also ensure that the media at least get something. Inevitably these solutions are not ideal. All reporters would like to have a one-to-one with the subject of the story. They would also be concerned when they only have the same information as everyone else. But at least it provides everyone with a story in a reasonably civilised manner.

Other options can mean the potential interviewee never talking to anyone and the press appearing to behave in a manner that is becoming increasingly unacceptable to ordinary people.

Reporters and photographers need to be careful about invading people's private property, something both the PCC and the BBC warn against. The PCC code of practice says that 'The use of long lens photography to take pictures of people in private places without their consent is unacceptable' (PCC 1999). It identifies a private place as somewhere 'where there is a reasonable expectation of privacy' (ibid.). This is particularly true of hospitals, according to the PCC code, but would also obviously apply to homes, hotel rooms and the homes of friends.

Misrepresentation

All UK ethical codes of practice also warn against reporters pretending to be someone else, misrepresenting themselves, unless there is a real public interest. Pretending to be a police officer is specifically illegal, but borrowing a white coat and stethoscope to pretend to be a doctor, for instance, is just as bad, ethically. The same is true of using hidden cameras or microphones. The PCC code specifically bans the use of 'clandestine listening devices' (ibid.) or phone tapping. The BBC has a long passage in its producer guidelines about the use of hidden cameras or microphones without consent. The story would have to have a strong public interest defence for it to go ahead.

Protection of sources

When we promise a source that we will not reveal their identity, this is a promise we are obliged to keep. A source may be telling us information that could lose them their job, or even their life. But of course you don't have to promise to keep a source's identity confidential if you don't want to, provided you understand that the source may well then refuse to talk to you. This may be acceptable because a story without the name of the source may not be of much use. The only reason for promising confidentiality is because it is the only way you will find out about the story. You will then have to worry about how to source it properly, later on. It is possible that a court in the UK might try to force you to reveal a confidential source and several British journalists have been punished by the courts for this type of contempt in the past.

The BBC, NUJ and PCC codes of conduct all remind journalists of their obligation to keep confidential sources of information confidential.

In practice it is extremely rare for a journalist to promise confidentiality to a source because you will need to use their material in the story and will want to name them. If their position is so sensitive that secrecy is imperative, you will need to agree this from the beginning. You will need to be certain that the story is worth it and to do that you will need to get some idea about the story from the contact. Having decided the story is important enough to risk proceeding with a promise to keep the source's identity secret, it is important that you are very careful about collecting documents from the source or anything that might identify the source. The courts could insist on you handing over this evidence and it would be an offence to destroy or dispose of it.

Notes or evidence from a confidential source should be kept separate from general material so that it can either be destroyed as soon as the story is published or sent somewhere for safekeeping where you no longer have control over its availability.

Protecting notes, pictures and sources

Just because you haven't promised confidentiality to a source, however, doesn't mean that you don't want to protect information, people or contacts that you did not use in the published story. It is possible that the police or others will try to get you to show them notes, pictures or contact names that were not published. You have a duty to the source, not of confidentiality (unless you promised that) but certainly of privacy. If you did not need the information for the story, and therefore did not publish it, you should keep it private. If the police seek to force you to reveal the information, this could compromise your future activities. If people get the idea that journalists freely allow the police to trawl through unpublished material, photographers and reporters may find their safety, occasionally their lives, put at risk. If every protester or rioter knows the police will be shown unpublished pictures or video, journalists may well find they are not safe to cover such events as they will be seen as police informers.

The BBC insists that a court order is obtained before such material will be shown to the police and others have followed suit. Journalists are not there to act as an investigation unit of the police (although they may do that job on occasion, after exposing wrong-doing). Journalists do not have the protections afforded to the police and if they are to keep people informed of events, they need to be sure they are safe while so doing and are not seen as an extension of the authorities.

SECURITY

Some places that you will go for stories require particular security measures. Coverage of royal visits, for instance, is limited to reporters who are on the royal rota. This system limits the number of reporters and photographers and obliges those given a pass to share their copy and pictures at specified rates. Rota passes for newspapers are arranged through the Newspaper Society (www.newspapersov.org.uk/nsservices/royal-rota/royal-rota.html Feb 2001) and your news editor should have done this if he or she wants you to cover a royal visit. Party conferences and many other big governmental conferences also require you to apply for a press pass some time in advance. For everyday identification you may already have a press card issued by the national press card scheme. If not, you can apply for one through one of several organisations. The National Union of Journalists is one of the scheme's 'gatekeepers' and authorises several thousand cards a year to members, staff and freelance. The Newspaper Society and The Newspaper Proprietors Association also authorise cards to journalists working in the newsrooms of their members. It is usually worth ringing the press office of any organisation that is running a conference or meeting, big sporting event, major entertainment event and so on and checking whether you need a pass and whether you can have one.

8

Inside the door

You've identified your story, you've decided where to go and who to see in order to get the information, now you're all ready to get out there and get your story.

TAKING NOTES

It's not much good doing a brilliant interview if you can't remember a word of it once you step outside the door. Some form of system is required to ensure that you are able to remember what was said in order to write the story and also prove that it was said in case of later dispute. A court hearing a defamation action, for instance, might require evidence that the interviewee said what you claimed. More routinely, your editor might also require such evidence. If the interview is for broadcast, then there will be some sort of tape, whether audio or video, and this will be sufficient for both the court and your editor. Make sure original tapes, of contentious interviews at least, are kept for a minimum of a year. Broadcasters are obliged to keep tapes of transmissions, but not for long enough to protect against a defamation action.

Because tape recording is so easy these days, it is often tempting for a reporter to tape an interview. Whilst Dictaphones can be useful on a one-to-one in-depth interview, they are of much less use for short interviews with a number of people. At the end of the day, a reporter's shorthand notebook is still the best and most efficient way of taking notes.

Tape recorders are prone to run out of batteries at the vital moment or need to have the cassette turned over. They often fail to pick up the sound of the interviewee unless you use a proper tie-clip microphone. I once interviewed the Swedish Press ombudsman in Stockholm using a tape recorder. We were alone in a quiet room and I anticipated no trouble, although fortunately I stuck with my habit of using a notebook as well. On leaving the office, I stopped at a café for a coffee and checked the tape. All her softly-spoken words were merely a dull, barely-audible fluttering. I could not make out a single word. My notes were just about good enough to give me what I wanted, fortunately, because it was not possible to repeat the interview.

You are often not allowed to use tape recorders; they are illegal in UK courts and many other public bodies ban their use. In any case, they are rarely any good at big meetings because of the noise. If you must use one at press conferences, put it in front of the PA speakers, not the actual person speaking. The final nail in the coffin of tape recorders as far as I am concerned is transcription. In order to write your copy, you need to listen to the whole tape – often stopping and starting it in order to transcribe choice quotes. If the interview or press conference you attended lasted thirty minutes, you can guarantee it will take at least forty-five minutes to write the story. Using a notebook, I could have written the whole story within ten minutes of finishing the interview. I could also phone copy over direct using my notebook, scribbling my intro in the book while waiting to be connected to copytakers and adding the rest direct from my notebook. A notebook is easy to use, cheap and unlikely to be stolen. Even if you lose it, it's probably not a disaster (unless you've got unwritten stories in it). Even if it is lost, it's likely still to be where you lost it, because who would take a notebook?

Using a notebook is simple. Write the date and the names of the people at the meeting at the top of a clean page together with a note of the story and then start writing notes to remind you of what is happening. Try to take verbatim notes of what people are saying. Most reporters develop some form of speed writing or learn shorthand.

Teeline shorthand is very popular as it is relatively easy to learn and can allow a proficient reporter to write at up to 150–160 words a minute. Most trainee reporters are expected to reach 100 words a minute and this is the speed the National Council for the Training of Journalists (NCTJ) insists on for its exams and it is the speed most editors require from new staff. Most university or FE courses that claim to prepare students for a career as a newspaper reporter will teach shorthand in some form.

The broadcast industry is less insistent on shorthand than the newspaper industry and most training courses for broadcast journalists no longer include it on the curriculum. Most broadcast interviews are recorded and broadcasters tend to produce only short reports of courts, council and parliament. Even a major court case is likely to be no more than a five-minute package on the main news bulletin – something a good reporter can easily cope with using their own speed writing, particularly as interviews are videoed or taped and so do not need to be noted.

Shorthand is particularly useful for the new reporter, who is still not certain what will be used in the report, or a reporter covering court, council and other long-running situations. Notes can be taken during debates or throughout the interview or press conference and then during the boring bits or in breaks, the reporter can quickly read through the notes and mark the interesting passages. This early editing of what has been said can really speed up the writing process. Many reporters draw a vertical line down the page, writing only on the right-hand side, leaving the left-hand column to make annotations. New reporters and students find note-taking difficult and so often abandon it to concentrate on conducting the interview. This is a waste of time because, of course, they cannot remember the interview after because they have become so flustered. Don't be afraid to take your time and write down the notes you need.

It is important to remember to ask the interviewee before starting the interview if it is OK to take notes or to record what they are saying. In legal terms, what the interviewee says is their copyright and we can only note or record it with their permission on the understanding that it will be used in a news item or feature. It would also be ethically wrong to record what someone is saying without their permission. However, should you accidentally record someone who had not given permission, but there were a public interest reason to use the material, you might get away with its use. 'This defence is not set out in the CPDA [Copyright Designs and Patents Act] 1988 but the courts have shown a willingness, in exceptional cases, to allow a defendant to avail himself of it' (Carey 1999: 106). John Major, while he was Prime Minister, famously referred to some of his Cabinet colleagues as 'bastards' while waiting in a TV studio for an interview to start. Whilst the interview had not started, taping was continuing from a previous interview. This story was clearly in the public interest and was widely published.

Good note-taking is vital to ensure the accuracy of your stories both in terms of using accurate quotes and noting down names, addresses and any figures accurately. Always double check names and figures with the person concerned.

Actually taking notes during an interview is not easy. A notebook can be intimidating for an interviewee not used to talking to the media. Slamming your notebook down on the desk and leaning over it while you scribble down everything they say is going to make them far more cautious. Sit back in your seat and rest your pad discretely on your lap. Crossing your legs can allow you to slant the notebook towards your hand and away from the interviewee allowing you to make full notes without being too obvious about it, allowing the interviewee to relax.

The same applies to tape recorders whether for note-taking or broadcast. Always ask if you can use the equipment and discuss with the interviewee where to put it. Cameras require the same courtesy, although it is usually the photographer or camera operator who will sort that out.

THE NEWS THEATRES

Courts, councils, inquests, press conferences and parliament are all routine theatres of news and each offers its own particular challenge. It is likely that, if you are working on a local paper or radio station, that you will regularly attend court or council. Inquests are a less-frequent occurrence.

Court

There are two main types of criminal court you are likely to end up covering. Magistrates courts and Crown courts. Magistrates courts are presided over by three Justices of the Peace – lay persons appointed by the Lord Chancellor. There are about 25,000 JPs in the country working part-time (usually two days a week) in about 1,000 courts (Crone 1995: 78), usually situated in larger towns. Because these JPs are not lawyers, they are assisted and advised by the court clerk, who is a qualified solicitor or barrister. He or she sits immediately in front of the JPs and ensures the smooth running of the court. Some larger Magistrates courts in big metropolitan areas are staffed by full-time stipendiary magistrates. These are qualified lawyers and generally sit alone whilst lay magistrates sit as a committee of three. The Magistrates courts deal with summary offences, such as careless driving, speeding or common assault or what are known as either-way offences. These are cases that can be tried in either a Magistrates court or a Crown court. Normally the choice will be that of the accused, who may wish to be tried by judge and jury. Sometimes the Magistrates court may transfer a case to Crown court because a Crown court can give harsher sentences. A Magistrates court is limited to imposing a fine of £5,000 or a jail sentence of six months for a single offence (Crone 1995: 79).

The Magistrates court also deals with bail applications and transfers to Crown court. When a person is charged with a serious offence, this must be heard in the Crown court. The Magistrates court usually hears the transfer procedure in private and the only way a reporter can hear about it is by reading the order of transfer on the court notice board.

If the defendant is charged with a serious offence, the police may decide to remand the suspect in custody. They must bring the person before the next available Magistrates court where an application for bail can be made. A Magistrates court can refuse to allow bail, holding the person on remand, if there are substantial grounds for believing the accused will:

- fail to appear at court in answer to bail; or

- commit further offences while on bail; or

- interfere with witnesses or obstruct the course of justice (Carey 1999: 27).

Most cases before magistrates are the minor day-to-day iniquities of modern urban living – motoring offences, drunkenness, small-time violence and petty theft.

Only if the offence is indictable does it go before the Crown court. There are four types of judge on each Crown court circuit. High court judges, who should be addressed as Mr Justice Jones or Mrs Justice Jones; circuit judges who are addressed in reports as Judge John Jones or Judge Joan Jones; or recorders or assistant recorders who must be barristers or solicitors of at least ten years' experience who are called the Recorder, Mr John Smith or Mrs Joan Smith. Barristers are usually the only people with right of audience in the Crown court and all cases are heard before a jury of 12 people.

The High court judges sit in the more important centres and must hear the most serious cases such as murders. They may also try cases of rape, unlawful killing and other serious crimes. Their archaic costumes and the importance of the court can make these awesome occasions.

If you are hearing a case in the Magistrates court, you will first need to find out in which court your case is being heard. Most courts contain several courtrooms and you will have to choose which you attend. In days past, newspapers might have several reporters at court, but it is more likely these days that you will have to go to court to get the court list (unless your local court is kind enough to post it on each week) and study it to see which, if any, cases you want to report. Most cases are listed in advance, but of course some involve incidents that happened over-night. If there has been a major incident, then you might need to turn up at court, otherwise a sympathetic worker in the court clerk's office might ring you, provided you have kept up close contact.

It can be tempting to try to cover courts without actually attending, but the law requires that if you cover a court case, that you do so in a fair and balanced way and this is difficult to do with a bare bones report of the charge, the verdict and the sentence. Fewer newspapers use news reports from Magistrates courts these days and radio reporters are rarely there. However, an interesting sounding case will come up occasionally. Most Magistrates courts have a press bench and you should find out where it is if you don't already know. It is permissible to come and go during a trial, but it is polite to wait for a suitable occasion – a gap in proceedings or the end of a case. Sitting at the press bench offers no direct benefits, but it does allow the court to know the press is there and if the clerk decides to offer you some papers or copies of material the court has seen, it is easier for them to do.

Once in court you should identify who is sitting on the bench. Once the case starts, the name of the defendant and the charges will be read out. You should confirm these against your court list. The prosecution will then outline its case, calling witnesses as required. Once finished, the defence can either claim no case has been made out, or, more usually, present its case, again calling such witnesses as required. Both sides then wind up and the magistrates decide on their verdict. If it is 'guilty', they will then need to decide on a sentence. They may then ask the defence to make a plea on sentence and a further short speech will be made, perhaps supported by witnesses such as a social worker, priest or teacher to give a character reference. The sentence will then usually be passed.

Occasionally, after a court case, someone, the defendant or a relative of the defendant, might ask you not to cover a case. Some of these pleas can be heart-rending, but all you can do is say you will pass the information on to the editor. The same is true if you are threatened. You must in both instances inform the editor that you were approached, and tell him or her what was said. It is the editor's decision whether to use copy or not.

If it is the magistrates who ask you not to cover the case then that is different. Magistrates can instruct the media not to identify participants under the age of eighteen, but any other attempt to postpone reports or exclude the press can normally only be done if there is a risk of prejudicing the trial. If you are excluded, ask for the section of the Act being applied and tell your editor immediately.

Once the trial is over, you will need to write up your story. In order to qualify for privilege – the system that allows you to report what was said in courts or council provided your report is fair, accurate and contemporaneous – you must publish as soon as possible. If the court case goes on for several days, you must ensure that you continue to cover it, in order to report it fairly. Reporting the first day, when the prosecution case is put, missing the next two days and then reporting the prosecution winding up and verdict would make for an unfair report and put you at risk.

There is no law preventing you from interviewing participants in trials once they are over and only the normal rules of sensitivity apply.

Interviewing jurors at Crown court can be more delicate. It is illegal to ask them about their deliberations and what took place in the jury room whilst they were making their decision. To report one juror saying that another said,

'I knew he were a wrong'un from the start – his eyes were too close together' would be an offence, while reporting on whether the juror enjoyed the experience of deciding a fellow human's fate might not be. Some lawyers believe that naming a juror could put a reporter at risk of contempt of court as it could put a juror at risk of intimidation or attack (Welsh and Greenwood 1995: 43). There have been no prosecutions that I am aware of but on the other hand such interviews are rare.

The Crown court is altogether more daunting than the Magistrates court. Trials go on much longer for a start, requiring careful concentration. It may be that you will have to pop out several times to transmit material to your newsdesk.

Again you should use the press bench in order to get a good seat, but one where constant comings and goings can be more easily masked. Some of the big trials see so much media interest these days that the courts set up special rooms. The Harold Shipman trial (in 2000) was held at Preston Crown court, as was the Jamie Bulger (1993) trial. Both saw hundreds of reporters in town. Special press rooms were set up so that media reporters could watch the trial on closed-circuit TV and had suitable places for press reporters to write up copy and then phone it through, and for TV reporters to produce pieces to camera.

Working in the precincts of any court with a still or video camera is against the law. Taking pictures or filming needs to be done away from the court. You might get away with doing it on the opposite side of the street with the court in the background, but it is probably better to try to find a building similar in design to the court and close to it and film there.

Remember that you should be respectful in court and avoid attracting the attention of the judge. Turn off your mobile phone or put it on to vibrate-only mode. Make sure it is set to divert calls to your voice mail so that you can pick up the message at a more convenient time. It is illegal to take pictures or use tape machines inside the court – even if you could tape record the proceedings, it is unlikely that the quality would be good enough to use. You must rely on your notebook and your shorthand.

Contempt

Any attempt to interfere with the courts and the administration of justice in the UK is called *contempt of court*. This is taken very seriously by the courts and offenders face large fines or even prison. The law in the UK takes the view that the accused is innocent until proven guilty and that a fair trial requires that the courts and the jury have not been previously prejudiced against the defendant. In the UK it has been agreed over the years that the easiest way to do this is to prevent the media publishing anything other than standard details about alleged offenders.

There are now two offences of contempt:

- Strict liability – as defined by the Contempt of Court Act 1981.

- The old common law offence of contempt.

Strict liability is defined by the Act. It means that the prosecution no longer needs to prove that the defendant intended to prejudice the trial as would be the case under common law contempt. The prosecutor only needs to prove that there was a substantial risk of prejudice in 'active' proceedings. In the Harold Shipman trial, for instance, a radio DJ broadcasting in the Preston area, where the trial was being held, said on air during the trial that Shipman was 'as guilty as sin' and should own up in order to save the cost of the trial. He was obliged to face the court and was given a strict dressing down by the judge. Fortunately, no members of the jury had heard the radio programme, otherwise punishment might have been much more severe. Proceedings are normally considered to be active once someone has been arrested or a warrant for arrest has been issued (see *Press Gazette* 4/2/00: 1).

Council

Council meetings are also set-piece situations. There are several types of council meeting in England and Wales and you may attend all of them at some time in your career. Scotland has its own parliament and so much of the local government system is structured differently.

County councils control the English counties. There are also district councils that control parts of counties, unitary authorities (they have the powers of counties and districts) and London borough councils. There is also the Common Council of the City of London and the Council of the Isles of Scilly. In Wales there are county councils or county borough councils.

County councils are traditionally responsible for things such as transport, education, social services and the fire brigade. The police come under the auspices of their own Police Authority, a mix of local authority representatives and independent people appointed on the authority of the Home Office. District or borough councils traditionally control such activities as housing, planning, roads, street lighting, waste collection, parks and gardens and leisure activities. The National Health Service and hospitals are administered by health trusts. Parish councils (community councils in Wales) are the smallest councils and these control small amounts of spending on local activities.

According to the Local Government Act 2000 all councils have the power to do anything that they think will promote or improve the economic, social or environmental well-being of their area. Every local authority is obliged to prepare a 'community strategy' that explains how they intend to do this.

Local authorities are made up of councillors – local people elected by local people to run the business of the council. They are elected every four years and are usually members of one of the main political parties. Occasionally some councillors are independent or belong to a local 'ratepayers' party. There are three election methods. In one, all the councillors retire every four years and new elections are held. In the next, half the councillors retire every two years and new elections are held, in the third, elections are held every year other than the third year and one third of the councillors retire each year.

The Local Government Act 2000 introduced a number of changes in the way local government works. Rather than have committees and sub-committees overseeing the council's work with regular council meetings to review it, the local council will change to a cabinet style of operation by 2003 with a 'local authority executive'. This means that either there will be a:

1. directly-elected mayor who will appoint an executive of two or more councillors;

2. a council leader elected from and by the elected councillors with an executive of two or more councillors appointed either by the leader or by the local authority;

3. a directly-elected mayor and a council manager appointed by the local authority, or;

4. an executive directly elected by the electors to either specific or non-specific executive posts.

If a local authority chooses any style of executive other than a council leader, then a referendum is required of local electors. No executive will be allowed to have more than ten members, including the mayor or leader.

The executive will then have its decisions overseen by an overview and scrutiny committee. This will have the power to recommend either that the unimplemented decision be reconsidered by the person who made it or that the decision should be reviewed by the local authority. Neither the overview committee nor the executive is required to apply section 15 of the Local Government and Housing Act 1989 which makes it a duty to allocate seats to political parties in a balanced way.

In practice this is likely to mean that the council's policies and actions will be controlled by the mayor, the executive, a member of the executive or a committee of the executive or by an officer of the authority. The executive can decide which of its meetings to hold in private subject to regulations to be issued by the Secretary of State.

Whichever of these options the local authority opts for, the councillors will then meet about four times a year to oversee and scrutinise the work of the mayor or council leader and his or her cabinet. The meetings will be chaired by the local authority chairman or vice-chairman neither of whom are allowed to be in the executive.

Each local authority is obliged to draw up a code of conduct and have a standards committee that will promote and maintain high standards of conduct. There will also be a Standards Board for England and Commission for Local Administration in Wales which will monitor and advise on standards of conduct in their areas. They will have ethical standards officers to investigate complaints and monitor local authority conduct.

Each local authority has to keep a register of members' interests and this is available for scrutiny by any member of the public. Any local government reporter is going to need to visit this register for a serious session.

Elections

Elections make for good stories. More and more people are becoming cynical about politics and local elections are not taken very seriously despite the fact that local councils deal with millions of pounds of taxpayers' money. Nevertheless, reporting on elections is still important. Newspapers have a pretty free hand about the way they cover elections provided they don't print false statements. They can be partisan and decide to support any party they choose. They are not obliged to give equal coverage to the various parties, although many local papers choose to as a matter of policy. Broadcasters do have to be fair (Representation of the People Act 1983). The law says that they should give balanced coverage to the various candidates over the period of the election.

Election coverage can be fun. You will need to keep in touch with the various candidates and in a parliamentary general election there are likely to be daily briefings from the parties at national and local level. Each party will try to lead the agenda – to control what is published or broadcast – but of course it is important that you try to ensure the candidates are obliged to keep to the issues you think are important. This is particularly true of local reporting where the big issue for your constituency may be very different to the line the main parties are attempting to follow nationally.

The actual election count will usually be held on the night of the election. Most polling ends at 10 p.m. and the ballot boxes are swiftly whisked off to a central point in the constituency to be counted. This may be the hall of a local school or a community hall of some kind. The introduction of proportional representation and party list seats for Northern Ireland, Scotland and Wales makes some of our elections a little more complicated, but most are straightforward, first-past-the-post elections in which each elector gets one vote and has to choose one candidate. First ballot papers are sorted by candidate and any in which the voter's intentions are not clear are removed – there are usually only a few of these 'spoilt' papers. Then they are sorted by choice of candidate and bundled together in hundreds. It is then relatively easy to count the bundles and declare a winner. If the election is a one-horse race, then this is often obvious from the start as the bundles are in plain view. However, once the count is started, you cannot leave the building and return and so filing copy at this stage is not easy (although you might get away with a text message from your mobile).

If the votes are very close, then a recount might be called. Initially this would just mean counting the bundles, but could eventually mean checking each bundle to ensure there are no wrong votes and that each bundle is complete. No matter how close the vote, it is unlikely that a compact urban parliamentary seat will take longer than three or four hours to count and recount and many parliamentary seats vie with each other to be the first to announce their result at a general election, with several declaring around 11 p.m. These results, of course, are pounced upon by the statisticians and fed into the computer to try to determine the likely national position.

Each parliamentary seat announces its votes straight after the count. The Acting Returning Officer (usually the council chief executive or a similar senior local government officer) will announce the result in the hall or on the town hall balcony (should they have such a luxury). The results are then pinned up at key points around the town.

Commercial organisations

Business reporting is important at local and national level. People need jobs and this requires organisations to provide them. In the UK and most of the Western world, it is business that provides many of these jobs and so the health of a particular business can be paramount to a local or national community. The news that Vauxhall were intending to close a car plant in Luton shortly before Christmas 2000 was big news and received headline coverage in newspapers and on TV. A story involving a major international company and potential financial hardship for thousands, particularly in the week before Christmas, shows the importance of keeping in touch with the business world.

Each business is owned by shareholders and run by a board of directors. These are people chosen by the shareholders at the annual meeting. A director is normally a person with considerable business experience who is seen by the shareholders as the right person to decide company policy and strategy. A director may well be on the board of several companies.

Shareholders own the company by buying shares. These may be publicly quoted and are then bought and sold on the Stock Exchange. The price of shares will rise and fall depending on the performance of the company and the general estimate of future profitability. Companies that are seen to have a bright future, even if they are not presently profitable, may have a high value. This is what happened to Dotcom companies such as boo.com in the very late 1990s. Although they were deeply unprofitable, most investors believed they were the future and bought heavily, inflating the price of shares enormously. As it became obvious that profits were not going to come until much later than first thought, and that such companies would need to be propped up by shareholders for far longer, the price of shares started to fall as people sold up to move into businesses that were more profitable. This forced many early Dotcoms to go out of business.

The directors are paid a fee for their services. Some directors are described as non-executive. These are directors who do not work full-time for the company. They attend board meetings and give the company the benefit of their experience and contacts. Many a former Minister of the Crown has become a director of several companies after leaving office because companies welcome the chance to have a director so much in the know. Parliament's standards committee has strict rules about how soon ministers may join the board of companies they have dealt with while in office in order to minimise corruption.

Other directors are employed full-time by the company. These include the managing director and there may be other directors such as the sales director, finance director or marketing director. The board is led by the chairman who can be either executive or non-executive. Most big and even medium-sized companies these days have press offices, or at least a communications department, and they are often the best starting point for enquiries. It is their job to know who to contact in the company to get the best quality information and they are often able to do a lot of your basic research for you. As always, of course, you need to remember that they are only telling you what is good for (or at least not damaging to) the company.

Companies are obliged by law to lodge details of their financial dealings and their directors on an annual basis with Companies House. These records can be searched by anyone to gather basic details of the company's financial situation, what it owns and who its directors are. Directors must also give their private addresses. Companies House is on the web (www.companies-house.gov.uk) and you can access very basic details there as well as a list of disqualified directors who are forbidden by law to hold any future directorships.

Companies that have failed are often insolvent – they have gone bust. These insolvencies are also listed on the web and the site can be worth checking from time to time (www.insolvency.co.uk).

Companies hold annual shareholders' meetings to report on how business is going and to elect or re-elect directors. Normally these are dull affairs but occasionally, if the company is going through a difficult patch, they may be worth attending. The company is not obliged to let you in, but you can still doorstep the meeting in order to try to talk to disaffected shareholders.

The company also issues an annual report and you should be able to get hold of a copy of this. It will contain the annual accounts as well as reports from the chairman of the board and the managing director.

Quangos and NGOs

Quangos and NGOs are quasi-autonomous agencies with a committee of lay people set up by government or international bodies to regulate, investigate or advise on any number of things. There are a large number of international NGOs, more than 1,000 non-departmental public bodies (NDPBs) in the UK, about 500 National Health Service Trusts, Authorities and Boards and a small number of nationalised industries, public corporations and other health-related public bodies, all with committees of the great and good who are paid to attend one or two meetings a month. These quangos range from the Advertising Standards Authority to the Zoos Forum. Many of the roles that used to be carried out by local authorities are now dealt with by quangos. These include the police authorities, health boards and various regulatory bodies that oversee transport, water, electricity and gas. There are far too many quangos to list here, but there is a web site at www.cabinet-office.gov.uk/quango. Whatever story you are working on, there may well be a quango with some official involvement, whether it's health, water or fuel, all with potential contacts to comment on the story. Often those serving on quangos are knowledgeable about the subject and so, although they may not be directly involved, they can be useful sources.

Charitable and voluntary organisations

When people are not at work they are often carrying out some sort of charitable or voluntary work. This could cover anything from a fund-raising dinner for a local school to a meeting of the local train-spotters' club, the London Marathon to an amateur dramatics club. All are potential story sources with leisure activities playing an important part of community life. Most charities and voluntary organisations are run by a committee of enthusiasts with a chairman, a secretary, a treasurer and other such officers as are felt necessary. A football club might have a fixtures secretary, for instance, while a photographic society might well have a competitions officer. The committee, usually of six to ten people, is elected at the annual meeting (often called the Annual General Meeting or AGM) by those members of the organisation who bother to turn up. Most annual meetings are dull affairs and it is usually sufficient to ask the secretary to send you a list of the officers elected after the meeting and details of any business.

There are several ways of generating contact with such groups. If you do not already have a record, you can find the names of the secretaries of many local voluntary groups and charities by visiting the local library. Notice boards and the voluntary register can often provide the vital contact. The Citizens' Advice Bureau sometimes has names as well. Some charities and voluntary groups can be tracked down through their web site. Although these are usually national, if you are after a local contact they make a useful starting point.

Trade unions

Trade unions are national collectives of workers in the same trade or profession, working together to protect and advance their working conditions and rates of pay. Only by combining together can most workers gather sufficient bargaining power to convince an employer that they should have better working conditions or wages. Journalists belong to the National Union of Journalists.

Although most unions are nationally based, for many people their main contact is with the work place collective. This may be a local branch or shop (although for members of the National Union of Journalists, it is called, rather quaintly, a chapel). These are led by a shop steward or branch committee. An NUJ chapel is led by a Father or Mother of Chapel (F/MoC). Work place collectives are often gathered into branches, although if the employer is big enough, that work place might also be a branch. This means that most unions have a three-tier structure: local (led by a shop steward and works committee), regional or district branch (led by a branch secretary, chair and committee) and national (led by the president, general secretary and National Executive Committee).

A considerable number of Acts of Parliament have been produced over the last 150 years to constrain trade unions or offer them privileges. The law lays down labyrinthine conditions on how unions should control their activities: who can be president or general secretary, the conditions that apply to this, how many people can picket outside a work place, and so on.

But the main rights are the right to belong to a trade union, the right for that union to seek recognition and bargaining rights with the employer and the right of people to withdraw their labour (go on strike) in pursuit of a grievance over working conditions or pay. Essentially, at present, if trade union members in an identifiable work place vote by a majority in a secret ballot to go on strike, that strike is legal and the employer is not allowed to sack anyone who fails to turn up to work.

Most trade unions are much more media savvy these days than used to be the case and their national office will have a web site and a press office. Some of the bigger unions will also have large regional offices, particularly in areas where a large number of their members work.

Often the local union officers at a work place are volunteers – activists who work in the factory or office and are members of the local committee. These are the people you really need to know, but of course they tend to change regularly, moving to other jobs, or different activities. If there is a regional office, it is more likely that this will be staffed by full-time officers, employed and paid by the union as experts in trade union organisation to support the lay activists. These change less often and so should also be in your contact book. The national office of a union with a particular influence may also be a regular contact. If you work at a major seaport, for instance, you may want to keep in touch with the press office of the RMT – Rail, Maritime and Transport union.

Press conferences

Press conferences are called by a number of organisations: a local council wanting to announce its new anti-litter policy, a company launching a new product, or a campaign group launching a crusade. Some press conferences are regular briefings, such as 10 Downing Street's daily briefings. Some are called just for a specific event – a product launch or a policy announcement. Attendance at press conferences is not obligatory and it is up to your news editor to decide if you should cover any particular press conference. If your news editor does send you then it is important to make the best use of the conference to try to get your questions answered.

MAKING PROMISES

Occasionally a contact will ask you to do something for them. If it is just a question of sending a copy of the paper then you can either agree or make an excuse. If you promise something to a contact though, you *must* carry it out. How can you expect them to trust you over something important such as protecting a source if you can't even be trusted to send them a paper?

Other requests may not be so simple. Missing out people's names from stories, not carrying stories or erasing quotes given and taken in good faith are all things that you may be asked to do. Never promise to do what is asked. Say you will raise it with the editor and that is up to him or her. Editors are there to take some of the flack. If you are propositioned in such a way, report it immediately to your news editor or editor and then follow their instructions.

Occasionally you may be asked to provide a copy of what you have written for the interviewee's perusal before publication. Whilst reading someone's quotes over the phone to them may on occasion be justifiable, providing a copy of what is to appear in the paper is never right. Apart from anything else, no-one can ever resist the chance to treat it as proof copy and to ask for alterations. Again you should refer such requests to the editor pointing out to whoever asked you for the copy that it is not policy and could get you the sack. It is becoming the norm these days for big celebrities to demand copy approval before granting an interview. Again this is a decision your editor will need to take; is the publication going to act as a PR arm for the celebrity or risk losing the interview? The biggest magazines, newspapers and TV can afford to refuse, but many of the smaller ones often feel obliged to accept.

9
Interviewing

Interviewing is one of the most important skills of the reporter because this is the tool you use to get witnesses to give their impressions and evidence. Any reporter who hopes to do a good job should be able to talk to an interviewee, quickly making them feel comfortable and willing to talk. If the interviewee does not trust the interviewer to deal with them fairly then they will not talk as freely as they would otherwise, so it is vital to build a relationship of trust as quickly as possible, even if the interview is little more than a grabbed couple of questions from a fleeing figure out on a rainy street.

WHAT THE PUBLIC EXPECTS

The public's view of reporters often seems to be coloured by the reporters of fiction. This impression comes from films and TV where reporters are played as unpleasant in order to build the moral uprightness of the hero. Even when the reporter is one of the main characters, there is often more drama in making them unsympathetic. This almost always means that the reporter is seen as someone who is either self-obsessed or rude and overbearing. Michael Elphick, for instance, starred in the TV series *Harry* as the eponymous freelance reporter who seems to have no real redeeming features at all. John Gordon Sinclair starred as Nelson in *Nelson's Column* – playing a reporter whose selfishness and ambition were the keys to the comedy, whilst reporters in *Drop the Dead Donkey* and *Hot Metal* were all deeply-flawed human beings. Since on their first contact with the media, the interviewee may also, as Keeble points out, feel intimidated by this 'awesome and seemingly powerful institution, the press, so capable of destroying reputations' (Keeble, 1998: 69) they are often pleasantly surprised. Nearly all reporters are (or can be) polite, even charming, human beings – at least for the length of the interview. The best quickly relax their subjects and soon make them feel able to confide their secrets.

TYPES OF INTERVIEW

There are two main types of interview:

1. as research for a news story;

2. as a performance; part of the story in its own right (mainly for broadcast).

It is important not to confuse the research interview for a news story with the performance interview for a TV or radio bulletin. The kind of adversarial interview by Jeremy Paxman for *Newsnight* is completely different to the interview you might carry out with the same politician for the same story, but off-camera or microphone. Many young and inexperienced reporters fall into the trap of believing that a research interview is the same as the performance and that a hectoring, intrusive manner is required. This is likely to lose you the interviewee very quickly and will certainly not encourage them to tell you anything useful. Even as a performance it is not always productive and several top-notch professionals, including Sir Robin Day, have had interviewees walk out on them (although of course this can be a good result in terms of TV drama).

There are several different types of research interview used by reporters.

- *The formal, arranged press conference interview.* This allows many reporters to interview one or more persons at once. It has the advantage of being efficient for the interviewee, but is limiting for the reporter as all media get the same material.

- *The one-to-one short interview.* Short conversations with police officers, emergency workers and plant operatives. None of these are long (the interviewees are too busy for long conversations) and they are focused on specifics, but they can still be useful for pointing up issues and adding colour. They can involve speaking to a number of people. These types of interviews are most likely to be done face-to-face but are also often done on the phone, or possibly by e-mail.

- *The one-to-one interview.* This is the reporter speaking to one of the key people involved in a story. This could be a senior police officer or the most senior representative of a company. These are often difficult to arrange on a big story, as this is what all the reporters want and these people are busy. It can be done by phone or e-mail, as well as face-to-face.

- *The vox pop.* This involves speaking to a number of people and asking their opinion about an issue. Vox pops (derived from Latin meaning 'voice of the people') are still often used on TV or radio, but are less popular in newspapers than they used to be. People are asked their opinion on a burning question of the day such as, 'Should we join the euro?' It can be useful to add colour to an issue of this sort that is otherwise likely to be heavy going and full of quotes from dull but worthy politicians and economists.

- *The profile interview.* This is an in-depth, face-to-face interview that is likely to take time. Most likely to be used to research a feature or personal profile, it is certainly used to really get under the skin of the interviewee. It is almost impossible to do well over the phone, because of the inability to see all the non-verbal communication. An e-mail interview of this type would take even longer than a face-to-face interview but might be useful for someone geographically remote. The possibility of such a person using a PR to write their responses, or at least advise on them, makes this type of interview technique for a profile practically useless, but it might be all right for an in-depth feature or news interview.

YOUR APPROACH TO THE INTERVIEW

The interview starts outside the door. You need to be clear why you are there, what you are going to ask and what you want to know. You need to be appropriately dressed with the tools of your trade – notebooks, recorders or cameras discreetly out of sight. You should not be smoking, chewing gum or doing anything else that is likely to spark an adverse reaction. The trite, old phrase, 'There's never a second chance to make a first impression' is only annoying because it's true.

Interviewing allows you to find out the who, what, when, where, why and how of the story and retell in the words of those who know about it with conviction, credibility and authority. It is all very well for us to say that a chief constable has supported the decriminalisation of soft drugs, but we much prefer to hear it from the man's lips. A TV interview or blocks of quotes with a picture in the paper add credibility and authority. They also bring the story to life and add interest. Without good solid quotes to support what you write, your story will be thin and unbelievable, and will certainly not carry conviction either to the reader or to the High court judge who may be called upon to set a level of damages if your story is inadequate enough to end up in the courts.

The first thing to do for a good one-to-one interview is to carry out a little research. Read *Who's Who*; go to your library and get out the cuttings. Having some details of the subject at your fingertips is both flattering to them and important for you if only on a basic level; your interview is not going to go well if your first question is, 'Well, Prime Minister, what party do you represent?' It does not raise your standing in the eyes of the interviewee and is likely to lead to them cutting you short. But knowing that a politician once held directorships in certain companies might well give you the insight into a good story, allowing you to link that knowledge with a remark made by the interviewee that would otherwise be meaningless.

Having done your research on the subject (assuming you have the time), it is also often worth researching the venue for the interview. If, for instance, a Cabinet Minister is visiting and you are able to grab him for a few minutes for a private interview, it will make you look more efficient and give you the chance to cut out the opposition, if you are able to say, 'If we just go over here minister, there is a quiet office where we can talk.' This is where a local journalist can often outwit the nationals – provided you do your research first. This knowledge is vital to the radio and TV reporter who would prefer a bit of space in a quiet, controlled environment to make the most of the interview. As in all things, preparation is the key to success. You have researched the subject and the venue, now you need to be sure you are clear about what you want to know. It is no good blindly asking questions in the hope that you will strike it lucky and get a good story. You need to know what you are after.

If you are talking to the Minister for Industry, it is not much use talking about the health service, unless you are working in local media and the minister happens to also be your local MP. Instead you need to know as much as possible about industry, particularly local industry, and be aware of any controversial issues. Put yourself in the place of the reader: what would they want to know if the minister dropped into their house for a chat?

Try to prepare questions that get to the heart of the issue. You are not there specifically to embarrass the minister just to show how clever you are – although if he or she puts his or her foot in it, you can certainly make the most of it! You are trying to find out about the person, the policies and the plans. Your aim should be to give the reader a clear picture of what is happening that might affect their lives.

ASKING QUESTIONS

Having done your preparation, you are ready for the interview.

Start by being polite. Remember, people do not have to be interviewed – they can easily tell you to push off. Only courtesy and charm is likely to change their minds and so you need to practise these. The only person who can improve on this is you. Practise being charming to people (it's a skill after all) even if it is just your friends, parents or your partner/boyfriend/girlfriend. Watch guests on TV chat shows and copy the mannerisms of those you thought charming and witty. It's perfectly possible to pick this up as an act until it becomes automatic, everyday behaviour.

The first rule of civilised behaviour and courtesy is not to be late. Turning up late implies that you think yourself more important than the interviewee, and that they are not deserving of respect and so is not likely to improve your chances of a good story. The interviewee may no longer have time to talk to you and is unlikely to be as cooperative as if you had turned up on time. If they are late then, of course, you have no option but to take it in good part and accept their apologies.

I have already mentioned that it is a good idea to dress appropriately. Whatever we like to think, appearances are important. People are inclined to make snap judgements and someone with dirty hair, two days' stubble, smudged make-up, torn jeans and a grubby green sweater is not going to get as good an interview as someone clean, neat and well-groomed and dressed in a smart suit. Personal hygiene is vital – no-one likes talking to someone who smells as though they died three days before. Avoid eating garlic or spicy food for lunch, and if you smoke or drink then breath mints are a must.

It's also important to turn off your mobile phone before you start. Having your mobile ring during an interview can only be worsened by you answering it and effectively putting the interviewee on hold in his or her own home or office. Turn it off (remembering to turn it straight back on afterwards) or put it on silent profile so you know you received a call. Most phones these days have systems to let you know if you missed a call or have a message.

Start the interview off as you mean to go on by greeting all those present in a friendly but business-like manner: smile, nod, handshake and greeting, including your name. If everyone from the receptionist to the second in command finds you approachable and friendly, you will not find it so hard to get to see the great man or woman next time you call. This obviously applies to the interviewee as well, whether protected by a staff of thousands, or just a spouse answering the door.

Once you meet the interviewee, introduce yourself fully. 'My name is . . . from the *Anytime Reporter*, thank you for sparing the time to see me, I'm sorry to bother you like this', accompanied by a handshake, ensures direct contact with the interviewee.

It is important to offer to shake hands with the interviewee. Touching is an important part of an initial contact because it has an enormous affect on the interviewee's perception of you. In one experiment by psychologists, they found that students evaluated librarians who touched them briefly while handing back the library card much more favourably than clerks who did not touch (Knapp and Hall 1997: 297). It seems that touch can be 'functionally influential' (ibid.: 298). Too much touching too early can, of course, be counter productive and will be seen as over-familiar. Unless you know the contact well, just a straightforward handshake with your greeting is enough. You can use the handshake to weigh the person up. Markham identifies eight different types of personality who give themselves away in their handshake from the *cold fish* to the *finger-shake* (Markham 1993: 81). These early indications of personality type can help you to quickly work out what makes this person tick and allow you to decide more quickly how to handle the interview.

Once in with the interviewee, you should remember that you are on their territory. Unless you are meeting on neutral ground, a hotel or public building, you should assume that the office, room or home you are meeting in is theirs. Humans are very territorial animals and although you have been invited in, this does not give you carte blanche to do what you like.

Psychologists identify three types of territories: '*primary territories* are clearly the exclusive domain of the owner . . . they are guarded carefully against uninvited intruders . . . *secondary territories*, which are not as central to the daily life of the owner . . . *public territories* are available to almost anyone for temporary ownership' (Knapp and Hall 1997: 155). They warn us that even a temporary invasion of someone's primary territory will still be seen as a *violation*. Moving furniture or using items without permission on primary territory, such as someone's home or office, is likely to be perceived as an attempted *invasion* invoking a strong antipathetic reaction. Imagine how you would feel if you invited someone into your home or office and they started moving the furniture.

You should wait to be invited to sit down. It is probably OK to take off your coat, but it also doesn't hurt to ask the interviewee if he or she minds you removing your coat. Don't move the furniture around without at least asking. If the only other chair in the office is across the other side of the room ask if you can move it: 'Is it OK if I bring that chair over here and sit down?' I have a small office that I share with a colleague. It is our territory. We lock it when we leave it and we expect people to announce themselves when they enter, with a knock or a greeting. There is a spare chair in the office well-placed for a visitor to sit and talk to either of us. I am always amazed at the number of students, who, having come to see me, move the chair, despite the fact that there is not really anywhere to move it to. I am also amazed at how much it upsets me. Why don't they ask? Why do they need to move it? I know it's silly, but they'd find me much more cooperative if only they'd leave my chair alone.

You also need to ask permission to take notes or tape an interview. This is, in part at least, a realisation that what people say in interviews is their copyright and to record it needs their specific permission. From that permission flows the understanding that you can use their answers in a news report. If you are going to record a radio or TV interview then this is the time to mention it and explain that you will interview them on camera or recorder as soon as you've talked to them about the story.

Handling the interview

While no interviewee, in the UK and Western tradition at least, wants to spend ages setting the scene, a little ice-breaking in all but the most urgent of situations is an essential aid to good communication; a sort of throat-clearing that allows interviewer and interviewee to gather their thoughts and concentrate wholeheartedly on the business at hand. Offers of coffee, getting notebooks and papers out, assessing character and situation, arranging the scene, queries about the weather, etc., can all be got out of the way in this period, leaving you clear to get on with the interview.

I find one of the easiest ways to get people into the interview is to ask their name, address, occupation and phone number. This has two purposes: it guarantees you have that basic information should something happen – a fire alarm or whatever. It also eases the interviewee's nerves. Just as the TV quiz show *Who Wants To Be a Millionaire?* helps the contestant settle in by asking laughably easy questions up to the first £1,000, so your early questions should do the same. If their name is unusual, ask them to spell it out or even write it themselves in your notebook in capital letters. Trying to write Takitheodopoulis when spelt out by a man with a heavy Greek accent can lead to inaccuracy.

You must always be polite and sympathetic. It doesn't matter how probing or unwelcome your questions are, if it is asked with enough politeness and sympathy and with a smile in your voice, the person will often answer, particularly if you make it clear you are waiting politely for their sparkling response. People are so highly conditioned to respond to questions that no matter how much they may not want to answer, they often feel compelled to do so, unless we interrupt them. When an interviewee is holding something back, you can just sit there looking expectant. Often they will fill the vacuum that quickly forms by expanding on their answer. Although this rarely fools the experienced, who will merely say something they want to say rather than something you want them to say, it is amazing how often people will say a little more than they intended.

Whether for TV, radio or newspapers, your job is to persuade the person to talk in the hope that they will eventually say something worth hearing. It is your job to sift through half an hour of drivel to find the few seconds of gold that explains your story. This is why a shorthand notebook is of more value than a tape recorder. If you are working for print, you will then include that quote in the story. If for radio or TV, you will try to get them to say it again live for the tape recorder or video camera.

Try to build up a relationship with the person. They have to be confident that you are going to treat what they tell you sympathetically; they have to feel comfortable talking to you. Whilst they must dominate the conversation with you prodding them in the right direction with questions from time to time, you can often get someone to open up even further if you can relate a brief anecdote that shows a shared experience. The fellow-feeling that this can induce can often bring the best out of an interviewee. Most people feel most comfortable when the conversational load between two people is about 50/50. Take the balance too far one way and the person will feel that the other person isn't interested or that they are being marginalised. An interview is different in that the interviewee expects to talk more but you should still aim to talk about 30 per cent of the time, not just quizzing them with question after question, but talking to them and above all, listening to what they are saying. You don't want the interview to feel like an inquisition. Some interviewers are so keen to show how good they are, that they are asking the next question before the interviewee has finished answering the last one. Not only is this irritating, but it can confuse and fluster an interviewee. A major press conference when scores of reporters are yelling out questions rarely persuades the interviewee to open up – it's too easy just to ignore the barrage of questions and speak to the pre-prepared text. Some reporter's rapid-fire approach often has a similar effect.

A good interviewer is someone whom people trust and to whom they feel comfortable talking. Everyone likes a good listener. Small encouragements of the 'How exciting,' 'Did it really?', 'Now, I've never heard of that happening before' variety can persuade the interviewee of how interested you are. Our questions and conversational gambits need to prove that we are listening to what they are saying and that it interests us. Body language and eye contact can be extremely important in this dialogue. 'Nonverbal communication comprises 65 per cent of all communication' (Webbink 1986: 9). Some researchers put the figure even higher (Markham 1993: 68). While a lot of this non-verbal communication supports and contextualises verbal communication, it is also a useful tool to hold up your end of the conversation without speaking. Nods of the head, hand movements, gestures and facial expressions can all show encouragement and interest, and these are vital for a broadcast interview where verbal encouragement is not possible. Nods, smiles and head movements must replace the short affirmative comment. It's important to be aware of trying to do this while still remaining natural about it. Having built up a relationship in the research interview, this should carry over into the broadcast interview.

The temptation for the rookie reporter at an interview is to concentrate on note-taking, which means looking down into your lap. But this can give the interviewee the impression you are not interested. You also need to be looking at the interviewee in order to pick up the non-verbal cues they are offering you: 'nods or sweeps of the head, eye blinks, brow movements, and hand or finger movements occur in association with points of linguistic emphasis (Argyle and Kendon 1967, cited in Webbink 1986: 11). Establishing reasonable eye contact allows you to pick up the non-verbal cues and to offer some of your own to prove your interest. Some communications trainers, particularly those training sales people, favour a technique called 'mirroring', where the salesperson mirrors the body posture of the potential customer in order to appear to be on the same wavelength. This picks up on the widely observed phenomenon that people who get on well mirror each other's body posture. While it is important to listen and try to exude sympathy, mirroring can seem too artificial. As Markham warns: 'you would have to be extremely skilled to get away with it. If the other person were suddenly to become aware of what you were doing, he might think you were making fun of him and refuse to have anything more to do with you' (Markham 1993: 81).

Try to structure the interview so that your questions allow you to build a picture of the story, although there may be considerable detail that you will need to go back to. It is often best to let the interviewee tell you the story in their own words, unless they are one of those people who are easily distracted by their own thought processes. If you know that you have contentious questions to ask, these may be best left until the end. Get basic details first and then move on to the contentious issues. That way you won't come away empty-handed should the interviewee terminate the interview.

The vital thing to remember about interviews is that you must listen to what the person is saying. The whole point of the interview is to find out what the person thinks. If you don't listen during the interview, the interviewee may open up a whole new line of information and you will miss it. If you had been listening, then you can follow up this new line and perhaps get an even better story. It is for this reason that note taking must be a secondary occupation to listening and you must get into the habit of taking notes on autopilot, rewriting startling bits of information. Jot notes as the words come to your ears, while you concentrate on watching the interviewee and listening carefully to what they say. If what they say is brilliant, don't be afraid to say, 'Sorry, just a minute', and then write it down and rephrase any question you had. Markham talks about active listening which involves concentrating 'on what is being

said' offering 'feedback by paraphrasing or asking questions which indicate
that you understand what is being said' (Markham 1993: 77). She warns that
people with low self-esteem or the very shy often do not listen because they
are too busy worrying about what to say next, in case they make themselves
look foolish or in case people are looking at them (ibid.: 82). Offering feedback persuades the interviewee you are listening and have understood his or
her point of view; it also allows you to give the interview a more conversational style.

If you are also watching them properly, so that you can take account of their
body language and verbal style, you will often be able to tell when they feel
uncomfortable or under pressure. In some instances, this means you would
ease off, in others that you would press harder to give you the opportunity to
probe further.

Never be afraid to ask for further information, particularly if you did not
understand their answer. 'I'm sorry, I'm not quite sure I follow that, could you
go over it again?' or 'Let me see if I've got that right. You're saying . . .' are perfectly acceptable ways of double-checking information, particularly if it is
something new and possibly contentious. In my experience the apparently
silly question rarely is. Either the person has taken for granted that you know
more than you do or they have failed to explain properly.

Drawing the interview to an end should be relatively easy if you have
remained in control. Often it is worth asking a general question along the
lines of, 'Is there anything you'd like to add . . . ?' or 'I think I've got the full
picture now unless there's anything you think I've missed?'. Often people will
add a piece of information that you were completely unaware of. Once the
interview is over, it's time to go. Again politeness should be the rule. Thank
them for their time and shake hands again. It's worth remembering that the
interview isn't over until you've gone. Often the interviewee will relax as you
start to terminate the session. They may well politely escort you from the
premises and will continue talking. It is perfectly all right to continue interviewing. This is, after all, a continuation of your previous conversation.

Rules of engagement

There are a few rules of interviewing that journalists adhere to and which are
generally recognised by politicians, PRs and others who regularly mix with the
media.

Reporters talk about an interview being *on the record*. Anything said in such
an interview can be used and the person can be quoted. Unless someone says
anything to the contrary before the interview, you can assume any interview,

where you have told the interviewee who you are, is on the record. Although it might be wise to get the interviewee to sign a release if you are going to tape the interview for TV or radio, you can assume consent provided they knew who you were.

Off the record means that none of the material can be used directly in a story, although it could be used as background, i.e. as narrative in a story or for forcing attribution from elsewhere. Nor can you quote the source of the story. This tends to make the information useless. There's not much point in being told the local mayor is on the take if you can't use a source to say so. Don't feel forced to accept an off the record briefing if you don't want to. If you decide that you would rather seek another source than risk tying your hands with an off the record pledge, you can legitimately refuse to accept information off the record. This may mean, of course, that your interview is over.

Non-attributable interviews are only agreed to in certain circumstances. In this kind of interview, the quotes and information can be used, but not the interviewee's name. This leads to the use of phrases such as, 'A source close to Number 10', 'a well-informed source', and others. Unless the interviewee specifies beforehand that the interview is non-attributable or off the record, then it is on the record. It is no good someone being indiscreet and then trying to drag the indiscretion back. They must have your agreement that off the record is OK before proceeding. On the other hand, it might be wise to alert someone that your chat is on the record, especially if you know them fairly well.

Sometimes people will ask you for money to be interviewed. Unless you have a specific budget for this, just say you have no money and if they still refuse to talk, then try to find someone else. If they are the only contact, then seek advice from your news editor.

Telephone interviews

Telephone interviews are one of the standard ways of interviewing these days. It's so easy to be able to get in touch with someone quickly by phone. It's time-efficient, in that even if they live a long way away, you can conduct a twenty-minute interview and have the copy written within half-an-hour. No long journeys, no trying to find the venue, but also no face-to-face contact and no real chance to measure what the person is thinking. It's probably still better to interview face-to-face when you can, but these days it's often difficult to justify the time especially if all you want from that person is a specific piece of information or a confirmation. Radio, and to a lesser extent TV, find telephone interviews an acceptable alternative to the real thing. If you are unable to go out to interview the person and can't persuade them to come to the studio, the telephone is certainly the next best thing.

Using the phone can be a useful way of finding out who to speak to. If you are after a particular person then you will need to ask for them by name, but often you want to speak to the person responsible for a particular job and then the telephone can come into its own as the switchboard will usually be able to tell you who that is. You may not get directly to the person you are after. A switchboard operator and then a personal assistant might try to field your call. Always be polite but firm. If you are just seeking the answer to a question and the assistant can help, then that's fine, but if you need a quote from the boss then stick out for that. Whoever you speak to, make sure you get their name and job title. If what they said was contentious and they rang you, it might be advisable to find a number other than the one they gave you and check that they were who they claimed to be.

Using a phone gives you one major advantage. Hopper calls it *caller hegemony* (1992: 199). You make the call and the answerer takes a chance, because he or she doesn't know who is there and is obliged to interrupt other, possibly more important, activities in order to answer. How often have you halted something really important because the phone was ringing only to find out that it was someone trying to sell you double glazing or something else way down your list of priorities? You need to apologise to the person you are calling so that they realise you consider them as important as you and that they are not just someone you can interrupt with impunity. If the caller is busy or if your call has taken them by surprise, then provided deadlines permit, it may be worth quickly sketching out what you want to know and offering to call them back or let them call you so they have a chance to think through their answers before speaking to you. This will increase their trust. However, of course, it may also give them a chance to run away, so it is up to you to decide if you are better speaking to them straightaway.

When using the phone, you are not in a position to use body language, contact or gesture to help put over the message so you have to rely entirely on the pitch of the voice and your use of language. You need to be able to get your tone of voice to add all the body language you can no longer include. Don't be afraid to make your voice sound smiley. If you laugh, do it in a way that ensures the other person realises either that you were making a joke or that you understood what they said was a joke.

Always say clearly who you are in a friendly but firm way. Once you get to the person you want to interview repeat who you are and ask if it's OK to talk to them for a story you are working on. If you want to record the conversation then ask them if they mind. It is certainly bad practice, and arguably against the law, to record someone's conversation without their permission. On the phone it is even more important to leave the most difficult questions towards the end – it is too easy for someone to hang up.

If you use the phone for an interview it would be unethical to give the reader or viewer the impression that the interview was done face-to-face. The Press Complaints Commission warned in 1992 that such practices could give rise to complaints of publishing inaccurate and misleading material.

> In one article the reporter said of the interviewee: 'Watching her, sitting up in bed . . .' when in fact the reporter had never visited the house. This led the reader to understand that the reporter had been invited into the person's home when in fact what had really happened was that a short, and somewhat reluctant, telephone interview had been given.
>
> (PCC March 1992: 3)

Ringing back

If they have rung you back, then don't forget to thank them for taking the trouble to do that. If they promise to ring back, then don't rely on it. Often these promises are made by colleagues or assistants and the other person does not have the time or inclination to carry out a promise made by someone else. Leave it for a suitable period and then ring them again. Usually it's best to ask someone who promises to ring back, when the person you are trying to contact is expected so that you can ring them then. You don't want to keep ringing, wasting your time and the time of the person who has to answer your call, if the person you want to speak to will not be there.

E-mail interviews

E-mail interviews are a new method of finding information but can be very useful, especially if you want to interview someone abroad or in a different time zone. The huge advantage of e-mail is that you can send someone a message and they will respond when they are able, saving you the trouble of having to track them down or wake them up. But many people have e-mail addresses they only look at every few days and some people don't answer their e-mails for weeks. If you don't hear from someone after a few hours, it might be worth ringing them.

E-mails are also useful in that you can cut and paste the answer into your story ensuring that you don't accidentally pervert what the person said. E-mails are great for contacting experts who you have discovered on web sites. Perhaps you are doing a story about BSE and its possible effects on human health. You are bound to find a web site with the names of a number of experts. You can then e-mail them all and hopefully get some very usable quotes. Tracking down half-a-dozen university professors from all around the world by phone would take ages, but a group e-mail to addresses found on a web site is the work of a few minutes and can reap great results. Don't forget to make it clear you intend to use the results for publication. This is one time when you really have to be specific so that you are sure the interviewee understands how you intend to use their answer.

Always ask a string of questions in your initial e-mail. If you then have further questions, deal with those when you get a response. This saves a ping-pong approach that is long-winded by e-mail. It is better to be general so that the interviewee can give a wide-ranging answer. E-mail interviews are of less use for the 'How do you feel now that it's all over?' type question than the technically-based question about how something works. If you want to interview the victim of a rail crash, go and visit them. If you want to ask a professor of engineering about metal fatigue in rails, then e-mail may be the easiest method.

Interviewing difficult people

There may be people that you want to interview who simply don't want to speak to you or behave in a difficult manner if they do agree.

If after speaking to a person they don't want to talk to you, then there is no point in trying to bully them into it. You can certainly try to persuade them that it might be in their best interests to put their side of the story, but at the end of the day, people have as much right to keep quiet as they have to tell their story. Your major problem will normally be the news editor back at the office who is up against a tight deadline and wants the best story. Persuading him or her that you have done all you can to try to convince the person to speak without success is never easy. One way to get around this is to find a substitute. Who else can give the information that you were looking for? Even if the substitute is not quite as good as the original, being able to ring the news editor and say that whilst your first choice refused to speak, you have managed to get material from a reasonable substitute will usually get you off the hook. The news editor wants reasonable copy and if you've got it, he or she will be less worried about whether you are using precisely the contacts you promised. If the person you are after is the only person who can comment on that story then it might be worth pointing out that 'no comment' can often be very damaging and that some comment, no matter how anodyne, might be better.

Sometimes you meet people who are rude or abusive. There is no point in being rude back. Reporters often meet people who are under heavy stress. They are perhaps, being accused of wrong-doing, their lives are falling apart and it should be no surprise if the media is often blamed for this. Just console yourself with the thought that at least they can't chop off your head like messengers of yesteryear. Take a few deep breaths and respond as calmly as you can that you understand how they feel, but that it is your job to convey their views and feelings to others. Is this rage and abuse really how they want to be portrayed? This unaggressive but assertive approach often helps them recon-sider how they should handle you. Violence can on occasion be a problem, particularly if there is a press pack about. Being confronted by scores of reporters and photographers outside a building you are trying to leave in a hurry after a highly emotional confrontation can often lead to the person you want to speak to turning violent in their efforts to push through the crowd. Large crowds can be very threatening and in this kind of scenario it is hardly surprising if the person uses violence to try to escape. If it is possible to follow them without it turning into a hunt with scores of journalists pursuing a single car, then you might be able to approach the person later on when they have got over their panic.

Occasionally people will try to bully you into what they want written. Whilst it is OK for an interviewee to control what they are reported as saying – it's their words after all – it is up to you who else you speak to and what is said. It is important that you do not make promises you will be unable to keep such as saying you will not speak to a particular person, but otherwise it's worth trying to placate this sort of person by trying to appear to agree with them without committing yourself.

Sometimes an interviewee will try to find out what you know and will end up quizzing you. You must not allow that to happen and should turn the question back on them. Ask them how they feel about it or what do they know about it. Flatter them: 'You're the one in the know – what do *you* think about it?'

ETHICAL MATTERS

We need to remember that our contact with interviewees does mean that we have a duty to treat them fairly. Journalists should not normally use subterfuge or deception unless these are the *only* ways of getting a story that is in the public interest. If you wanted to interview someone about how they dealt in drugs, for instance, you might want to talk to them without revealing you are a reporter. This does not give you the right to buy drugs from them or pretend that you will – both would be offences and risk putting you in the same posi-tion as them.

A journalist should normally be both fair and honest with interviewees. It would be an abuse of trust to trick an interviewee into revelations they had not intended – unless the story is important and in the public interest.

While, as I said above, it is good sense to let the interviewee know who you are, it is also the ethical thing to do. When it comes to a broadcast performance interview, this is even more important. A good professional should do all he or she can to put the interviewee at ease. The interviewee should feel able to put their case as they want, and while it is fine for the interviewer to test that case and point out the criticisms that others may have made of it, it would not be treating the interviewee fairly to use the interviewer's skill and experience to pressure the interviewee.

I've often been an interviewee on radio in the UK over the years, talking about journalistic ethics. Some interviewers have attempted to make it look as though they are giving me a hard ride while others have been fair and straightforward, but have tested the case I have put forward by putting the other side of the story in a straightforward manner. Those seeking to show how clever they were, were always easy to trip up and provide weak and unconvincing radio. Those who were fair, but testing, usually built intelligent, useful discussions that helped me explain myself more clearly and helped their listeners understand the issues. They were also the hardest work.

One of the huge advantages broadcast has as a news medium is the ability to add context to a person's words. The sound of their voice or their picture and habitat can tell us a lot about a person. Interviewing a farmer about farming in his best suit in the studio, for instance, would not be as accurate as interviewing him in the cowshed in his working clothes, but if he had just been elected the local mayor, then he might prefer to wear a suit and his mayoral robes in the mayor's parlour.

Quotes

What people say has a particular magic for the consumer whether it is a local police officer, one of the victims of a rail crash or the Prime Minister launching the latest government initiative. While what people say can be heard accurately on the TV or radio broadcast, this isn't the case in newspapers. Broadcasters need to be careful about taking quotes out of context or using them in a different chronological order to reality. To quote a politician as saying, 'There may well be a case for legalising cannabis, but I have to say that I disagree with it' gives a completely different view of his political stance to editing that comment to say, 'There may well be a case for legalising cannabis . . .'. To use it in this way might be an accurate repetition of what the politician said, but it is an unfair and untruthful representation of the politician's views. This kind of misrepresentation can also be done by changing the order in which sentences are said – something both TV and print have been accused of in the past. If a journalist is reporting an hour-long leader's speech at one of the political conferences, then reporting the whole thing would lead to no readers or viewers. Journalists have the right and the duty to offer the highlights as they see them, but they must be fair to the original intention of the politician.

Sometimes, however, print journalists may decide to improve someone's grammar. This is not a problem for broadcasters. The way the person speaks is part of their personality and tells us a lot about them, but often what is said in the heat of a situation might sound fine on broadcast, but looks terrible in print. Double negatives, repetition and malapropisms are just some of the problems with everyday speech that you might consider changing before quoting someone in print. It's our job to tell the world what they think and feel, not to make them look foolish. This particularly applies to someone for whom English is not a first language.

Another trick that is widely used by journalists, especially if the interviewee is being difficult and will not get onto the story, is to ask the interviewee, 'Well, would you say that: "..."' and use what they said as an original quote. If the journalist understands that putting the witness's view into the words of the journalist is to risk exchanging truth for a sharper soundbite, then it may be a fair exchange. It is a decision every journalist interviewing an inarticulate witness has had to make.

Interviewing minors

Interviewing children or vulnerable adults is another ethical minefield. Both the Press Complaints Commission and the Broadcasting Standards Commission warn the journalist to only interview a minor with a responsible adult present. This is particularly true if the story is about the child's own welfare or the welfare of someone they know. Having said that, children can make good witnesses if interviewed properly. They are observant and are better at seeing what is actually there. They are, however, keen to please and will often say what they think you want them to say. It is important not to ask leading questions and not to express interest if the answers seem to be leading in a particular direction. Remember that being interviewed by a journalist, particularly for 'the telly' can seem unbelievably glamorous to a child and the risk is that they will try to impress the journalist with stories that simply cannot be true. Journalists also need to remember that there may be things that the child does not want to admit to when being interviewed in front of the teacher or parent. If they were a witness because they skipped school or were playing somewhere they shouldn't, they may well lie to you about it rather than get into trouble. There is no real way round this but not to use the material. You should not try to interview the child without the parent or teacher.

Research and cuttings

No journalist should use press cuttings to put together what amounts to a fictitious interview. Even if you believe that all the quotes gathered by others and brought together in the press cuttings library are accurate, you can't be sure that people haven't changed their minds. What we say at one point in time is often not the same as what we say another time.

The Press Complaints Commission warned journalists about manufacturing interviews in its March 1992 report:

> Cuttings are an essential part of newspaper research but too many journalists now seem to act in the belief that to copy from 10 old stories is better than to write a new one with confirmation by proper fresh enquiry. In one instance . . . a magazine admitted that because it had been unable to contact a woman who had been attacked by her husband some months previously, it wrote up the story on the basis of newspaper reports, inventing dialogue to put the story into the magazine's style. The result was an article which contained serious inaccuracies and was to a degree fictitious.
>
> (PCC 1992: 2)

10
Broadcasting
An introduction to radio and television
by Cecile Wright

The strength of broadcast media is the human voice, hearing, and seeing, for ourselves how people are feeling. We can judge their state of mind; whether they are angry, upset, elated, jubilant. We can hear the emotion in their voice, we can see it on their face, we can watch their body language and we can share in the moment as it is happening – a boast newspapers can never match. While the immediacy of the Internet may rival broadcast news, it cannot yet challenge the impact, the emotion and the intimacy of radio and television.

Radio makes pictures. Unlike television, which relies heavily on visual images to convey its message, in radio, pictures are created in our imagination. We can be stimulated through sound and voices. They signpost and shape our response, allowing us to create the visual symbols for ourselves. Radio is a very personal medium and allows the listener to take part in a way television, which is a very passive medium, cannot. It is relatively cheap to operate and therefore can offer greater access and participation to the amateur. It is simple, and it is fast – there is no waiting for the crew to arrive, a radio story can be on the air almost immediately. If there is a reporter on the scene all they need is a phone and their voice.

In June 1996 a massive bomb exploded in Manchester city centre following an IRA coded warning to a television station. While the BBC's television newsroom waited for the camera crew to get pictures back from the scene, its radio counterpart, GMR, had the story on air as it was happening. Radio reporter Richard Hemingway was on his way into the city centre to check out reports of a security scare when the device exploded. Using a mobile phone he was able to ring through to the newsroom and describe the moment he felt the blast 'hit [him] like a physical wall' as emergency sirens blared in the background. The emotion in his voice was evident and through his graphic verbal description we were able to picture the scene for ourselves.

While radio can create mental pictures, television must show them to us. It is picture-led and pictures must take primacy. The reporter must be confident that the story is a televisual one. A piece that works perfectly well in print, or on radio, may be unsuitable for television. It is not simply a question of whether it is a news story; the television reporter must also consider the visual interest and impact. The trap the television reporter must avoid is making radio with pictures. Television is not about producing what the BBC, in the early days of transmission, used to introduce as *an illustrated summary of the news*.

Former Prime Minister, Margaret Thatcher, said, 'The picture that comes into your living room is I think the most powerful form of communication known on this planet.'

You can argue that television is, at the same time, both the strongest and the weakest of the broadcast media. The advantage television has over radio is being able to show or demonstrate events, ideas and concepts. Seeing is believing, and the impact of advances in television technology is that we can now beam pictures from across the world almost instantaneously, allowing viewers to watch events unfolding before their eyes. But that reliance on pictures can, of course, also work to its disadvantage. If you haven't got the pictures, you haven't got the story. News values in television can be dictated by the visual impact of a story and good pictures can drive an item higher up the running order, while another may not make the programme at all because there are no pictures to illustrate it. They can detract, or distract us, from the story, particularly if they are poor, irrelevant or unimaginative. How many times have we seen television reporters using the same tired, old set-up shots of politicians strolling across Westminster Green at the Houses of Parliament?

Pictures can also alienate; graphic or shocking images may offend the viewer. Television cameras can be intrusive, and have led to accusations that television news is exploitative.

PLANNING THE STORY

In broadcast news getting it right at the planning stage can mean the difference between getting the item on air and missing the deadline. How the story is illustrated is vital in radio and television. You have to get to the scene to record the relevant sounds, known as *actuality*, or the pictures. Conducting an interview over the phone or in the studio will rarely produce the best coverage. So the more accessible a story, the more likely it is to make it onto air. This is especially true in television where the logistics are more cumbersome, more time consuming and more expensive.

The need for pictures in television may mean the reporter and crew shooting in several different locations for a single story, and when you have a fixed deadline to meet, time is of the essence. Wasted journeys due to inadequate or poor planning can jeopardise the reporter's ability to deliver the finished item on time. Clearly some stories can't be planned – a breaking story such as a bomb blast or a major flood – but these kinds of stories tell themselves; experience shows there will be no shortage of pictures. In most other cases it is not enough to simply turn up at the location and hope for the best. That's not to say you shouldn't always expect the unexpected; news happens, and the news angle will not always be obvious at the planning stage. Never box off a story *before* you have been out to cover it.

News coverage does not allow for the kind of full-scale planning expected for a documentary, but nevertheless it is necessary to have some idea of who and what the reporter will see when they arrive at a shoot. There's no point in arranging to film a trainee fire-fighter session for an item about the recruitment of women to the service, if on arrival it turns out to be an all-male training session. You will have wasted a day's filming, cost the newsroom a considerable amount in crewing fees, and incurred the wrath of the producer, who now has a hole in the programme yet to be filled. Few, if any, broadcast newsrooms can offer unlimited resources. News coverage in general is expensive, particularly television news, so on any given day there will never be more than a certain number of camera operators. The camera operator will be expected to shoot several different stories during the course of their shift and the news reporter rarely has the luxury of a crew to themselves for the day.

Planning is also important in ensuring the reporter will have sufficient time to return to base and script and edit the item in time for transmission. Knowing where they will be at a given time, what elements of the story will be picked up there, and which other locations they may need to visit, can help in estimating the length of time the shoot or recording will take overall. Some camera operators now also double as picture editors. They not only shoot the footage, but edit it as well. They know they must operate a cut-off point on the shoot that will give them time to get back to the edit suite and get the material ready for transmission. Of course, technology means it is possible to feed material directly from the location, in radio this allows the reporter to send back short news clips, *soundbites*, *wraps*, live interviews, or scripted voice pieces, *voicers*, for inclusion in bulletins. However, for longer or more detailed items, the reporter will need to have access to more sophisticated equipment and studio facilities. In TV, outside feed facilities can be costly and not all of them include editing facilities.

Radio reporting usually consists of a single person with a tape machine and that one person may see the story through from planning to transmission.

Currently in most television newsrooms the reporter continues to rely on the skills of a number of people to get the story on air. Without the input of the camera operator and the picture editor the television reporter cannot produce the finished story. The television crew may arrive at a story fresh from a previous assignment and may have only sketchy details. The reporter then is also expected to fulfil the roles of director and producer on the shoot. The reporter is the person responsible for pulling the story together and therefore must be the one to dictate the direction and treatment of the story. A good camera operator will have developed their own news sense and can, of course, be invaluable in offering advice and suggesting ideas – television is a team effort and the best teams work together.

But that is changing; increasingly television journalists are also expected to be technicians. Ever decreasing budgets for news-gathering operations mean cheaper and more efficient ways of maintaining coverage have to be found. For the generation of new journalists hoping to pursue a career in television, multi-skilling is the watchword for editors and managers. The advent of the video journalist means TV reporters are, like radio reporters, likely to become increasingly responsible for producing the piece from start to finish. New technology, significantly the advent of small cameras such as DV cams which are relatively inexpensive and produce broadcast quality pictures, means the picture gathering capabilities of news operations can be increased.

ITN in London introduced video journalists as part of its news team about three years ago. It currently employs twelve of them around the country to provide coverage in areas previously served by its regional bureaux. They tend to be journalists with around 1–2 years' reporting experience, or occasionally straight from college or university, who are given basic training in camera skills. Most see the job as a stepping stone to other positions. The video journalist is seen as a complementary resource to the conventional team of cameraman and reporter, and because they work from home as roving reporters they can very quickly be on the scene of a breaking story in their patch. It means if a journalist is first at the scene they don't have to wait for the crew to arrive; they can hang around to pick up footage from press conferences; or grab doorstep interviews which may involve long hours waiting for the subject to turn up. Few are used to provide primary coverage of major stories, or set-piece events, but using them to film various elements of a piece means the dedicated camera operator and reporter are free to chase the other main parts of the story.

Reporters in some regional commercial stations operate both as video journalists and are also being trained in the use of desktop editing. Bob Crampton, Executive Editor of News at HTV West, says only around one third of the material they broadcast is cut by a dedicated editor. The organisation intro-duced a digital desktop editing system, Editstar, four years ago when it revamped its newsroom operation. Video journalists now cut everything but the more sophisticated feature or sports coverage at their desk. Bob Crampton says that, while the system is unlikely to supersede the need for dedicated editors altogether, the big advantage is that it allows material to be turned around very quickly and frees up the professional editors to do more high-quality stuff. The drawback is the sound quality is inferior to analogue or Avid (another non-linear editing system). The predominant view in the industry is that while the new technology and the move towards multi-skilling is unlikely to eliminate the need for dedicated camera operators and picture editors, it is recognised that more and more material will be gathered and cut in this way.

THINKING ON THE MOVE

The broadcast journalist is always working against the clock, under the pres-sure of a looming deadline, so the ability to think on the move and be continually planning ahead is a valuable skill. A reporter should be thinking about the story prior to leaving the newsroom – a few preliminary calls can help establish what the story is about and the possible or likely angle the story may take. For the broadcast journalist, this is especially important. This way they can ensure they will get all the right elements. If a reporter returns to the newsroom without them, it is usually impossible to go back, and trying to compensate with sound effects, library pictures or actuality produced in the studio is extremely difficult and time consuming.

The demand for material about a story is constant, with many stations requir-ing updates every fifteen or thirty minutes, and in those organisations provid-ing twenty-four hours news, the demand is even greater. Even before leaving the newsroom to cover the story, a reporter may be asked to provide *holding copy*, brief details of the story so far which can be run until more detailed information and recorded material is available. The radio producer or editor may require a *voicer* over the phone, a *phono*, or *down the line* from the radio car as soon as more information has been gathered at the scene.

Recording or filming material in the order it will appear on air can save time, and the television reporter needs to keep track of what is being shot and approximately where it appears on the tape. The reporter needs to form a mental shot list, or jot down key images or phrases that will help them pin-point material quickly. When editing *up to the wire*, having some idea of where the required material can be found is vital. The competent and efficient reporter will be mentally writing a script in their head as they gather the material for the finished piece, the radio reporter will also make use of the time it takes to drive back to the newsroom. They will be reviewing the tapes and already have begun to edit the item in their head.

TELLING THE STORY

Telling the story in radio or television means getting to the action and capturing it on tape. Television reporting means showing not telling. A common mistake trainee journalists make is to think of television purely in terms of *talking heads*, the interviewees in the piece. Interviews are clearly important, but it's not enough to think of the pictures as *wallpaper*, or mere illustration, to cover the reporter's voice-over.

Radio must create pictures for us through sound. The radio reporter must capture the event or experience whole. Broadcast interviews are a vital tool but they can be predictable and boring. No story can be told through talking heads alone. The reporter must bring the story to life by recreating the outside world inside the listener's living room. Ambient sound, background noise, the sound of the action behind the voice, can be as important as the people involved in the story.

STORY TREATMENT

The principles of telling the story in both radio and television are essentially the same but with the added element of pictures. They can range from the copy story to the documentary.

A story that develops quickly is no problem for radio; it can get the breaking story on air more quickly than television because it doesn't have to rely on pictures. Radio stations can interrupt their schedules much more easily to provide on-the-spot reports on a breaking story.

Initially it may be no more than a headline – a brief summary of the main points. The update may become a copy story that gives more detail about the story without an interview, *actuality*. The *voicer* can be used to add further detail to the story once it becomes known. It may be written by a reporter chasing information over the phone from the newsroom, or may be fed live from the scene by a reporter who has not yet had time to gather any actuality. The live report from the scene can clearly add atmosphere and colour to the piece because it allows the reporter to add description and up-to-date information. The next step is for the reporter to find some actuality to add depth and an informed account or explanation of the story.

The actuality can then be used to provide a news clip or to produce a longer edited item – either a *wrap* or a *package*. A wrap is usually actuality combined with reporter voice-over between the clips. A package will be a more sophisticated piece using actuality, reporter voice-over, wildtrack and background actuality. The TV reporter will want to get dramatic pictures of the scene.

The grammar of television

A visual image can tell its own story and the benchmark for good television journalism is to let the pictures lead, words are minimal. The best reports are those that simply show us the pictures and let us judge for ourselves. Filmmaking has its own grammar, and pictures can be used in the same way as a writer uses words. The impact of a picture is not created simply by the image it shows, but the kind of shot used can also portray inflection, tone and meaning. For example, a developing shot such as a zoom or a pull out can highlight emotion, acting almost as an extension to the reporter's voice.

Television pictures work best when you visualise the action in sequences. Think logically how the pictures will relate to each other and will allow you to tell the story chronologically, taking the viewer to the action and following it through.

The opening shots of a television package are the most important. They are the introduction to the story; they must grab the attention and whet the appetite, as well as signposting the rest of the story. News is about action, so show us the event happening, moving, people doing.

Sound in a television piece is often neglected by the inexperienced reporter but it is a vital element. When filming for television, the camera microphone should always be live, even when shooting general views. Sound can be used to enhance emotion or create atmosphere. A lack of appropriate sound can weaken or devalue a piece; imagine a series of shots in a shipyard or a busy restaurant kitchen without any ambient or background noise.

The *piece to camera* is used for several reasons in a television item. It may be included to emphasise the immediacy of the news and to demonstrate to the viewer the organisation's presence at the scene. It may be included to compensate for an absence of pictures, in a court report for example, or to add additional information without the distraction of pictures. Often pictures and words may have to fight for prominence, and the pictures will usually win. If the voice-over is introducing or explaining complex information it is better to dispense with dramatic or interesting pictures and let the words take prominence. The piece to camera must be shot on location and should place the reporter against a backdrop of the action or scene. An item may begin with a piece to camera as an introduction to the story, or be used to tie together different threads of the story in the middle of the piece, or as a conclusion or sign off at the end.

Recording on location

The reason the broadcast journalist chooses to do an interview on location is to place the interviewee in context, and to create a sense of timing and place. The television reporter is also looking for a background setting with visual interest and one that will give a visual signposts to suggest who this interviewee is, why they have been chosen, what they are talking about.

The local water authority is warning that standpipes may have to be re-introduced due to a prolonged dry spell. The interview with the representative from the water authority should, if possible, be filmed beside a dried up reservoir, rather than in an office. It also saves time and resources to pick up two elements of the story at one location.

But if you had a doctor talking about the benefits of healthy eating and good diet it might make more sense to see him in the hospital restaurant or canteen than on the ward.

Filming and recording on location brings its own special problems. No location, other than a studio, will be acoustically perfect so it's important to be aware of distracting background noise and to ensure that ambient sound does not drown out the interviewee's voice.

- Is the background noise too loud – roaring traffic, aircraft flying overhead, men at work?

- Is the interview in an exposed location where wind noise will cause interference on the microphone?

- Listen for distractions, or background noise that can make editing difficult – piped music, a ticking clock, the hum from computers and photocopying machines in offices.

- Avoid large rooms because voices will echo around the room and the recording will be poor. If there is no choice then position the interviewee in a more secluded or protected position, maybe against the edge of the room or in front of curtains.

- Conducting an interview across a table or desk should also be avoided. It is difficult to create a relaxed atmosphere, the reporter will have to stretch and the voices will bounce off the hard surface.

If the recording is to include some ambient noise then hold the microphone further away from the interviewee and turn up the input recording levels. In order to reduce the level of ambient sound it is necessary to hold the microphone nearer to the interviewee. Always record two to three minutes of *wildtrack*, background and ambient sound at the scene. Wildtrack can be used to enhance a piece by adding atmosphere, it can be used to deceive by recreating atmosphere where none exists, or to repair by overlaying poor edits or material which lacks ambience. Every location, even an empty and seemingly silent room, will have ambient sound.

In a television interview the camera's role is to allow the viewer to watch what is taking place as unobtrusively as possible. The camera should be invisible, allowing the interviewee to communicate and interact with the interviewer. The interviewee should be framed so that they look and speak in the direction of the reporter and not at the camera. If they look directly at the camera they will appear to disregard or ignore the reporter and be directly addressing the audience. The interview should be framed with the participants almost opposite each other and close enough to hold a normal conversation; the interviewee should look across the frame into what is called *the looking space*, towards the reporter who is positioned slightly to one side. The eyelines in an interview should match, with the camera lens positioned just below the eyeline level.

In a piece to camera the reporter may be framed centrally, and will generally look into camera and directly address the audience.

The television interview should comprise of a series of shots: an establishing shot, or *set up shot* that can be a wide shot of the scene: the reporter chatting to the contributor, or the subject engaged in some activity such as addressing a class of children, testing substances in a laboratory, preparing breakfast or a cup of tea, something that puts them into context and gives a visual signpost of who or what they are; the contributor framed in *medium close up* for the interview; and *cutaways* to help you hide the joins. Cutaways are additional shots that allow you to edit the interview or the set up sequence without spoiling the illusion of a continuous coherent action or exchange. In a radio interview you can simply cut out extracts of an interview and join together the sentences, but if you were to do that in television while the sound may flow, the picture would jump from one position to another. The action either side of the edit must be replaced. This is where the use of cutaways is necessary. They can be close up shots of the action or a movement, for example a shot of hands or a computer keyboard, a reverse – where the reporter is seen nodding or listening; or pictures illustrating the interviewee's remarks can be laid over the speaker's voice.

After the interview always remember to play back the last fifteen or twenty seconds of the recording to make sure it is there.

THE BROADCAST INTERVIEW

The news interview is designed to let those involved in an event or issue tell the story in their own words so that the listener can judge for his or herself the validity of the argument or opinion. The interviewer's role then is to provoke or elicit such response by asking questions on behalf of the audience. The interviewer's opinion is irrelevant – their stance should be impartial and objective.

There are different ways of approaching an interview and it's important to establish what you are trying to achieve. The first questions the reporter should ask are: What type of interview am I looking for? Have I got the right person for the job?

Informational   The purpose of the informational interview is, not surprisingly, to provide information to the audience about a news story or event. It is usually short and to the point. It asks the key questions of who, what, where, when and how.

- *Who* did it happen to?

- *What* happened?

- *Where* did it happen?

- *When* did it happen?

- *Why/how* did it happen?

Emotional   The aim of the emotional interview is to allow the audience to share in someone's personal experience. Because the encounter is often intensely emotive this kind of interview is the most sensitive and intrusive, but it can be the most powerful and revealing.

Interpretative   The interpretative interview aims to analyse or evaluate what has happened. It can be a response to the events or an explanation of events. In both cases the aim is to put the event into context and examine why or how it has happened and the possible implications.

Adversarial or Accountable   It is in this type of interview that the reporter needs particularly to appear objective and impartial. The purpose of the interview is generally to allow someone in authority, or who is responsible for implementing policy or plans, to explain or justify their actions. The reporter may need to challenge or question these actions, and the danger is the interview may degenerate into a personal argument between the interviewer and the guest. It is not a personal confrontation. The reporter is there to ask those questions of interest or concern to the audience. Intimidating or overbearing questioning may provoke the audience to feel the interviewee is being unfairly treated, regardless of whether the issues being raised are justified and in the public interest.

While the newspaper reporter can remain anonymous to the audience, for the broadcast journalist there is no hiding place. The interview is a performance and the reporter is being scrutinised and judged as much as the interviewee. They must be seen to be in control, to be challenging or questioning, but not to be overbearing or intimidating; and that can be a difficult balance to achieve, whether faced with an inexperienced interviewee or an old hand.

In radio and television the interview is much more problematical than it is for the press. Where the print journalist can compensate for the nervous, hesitant or reluctant interviewee, the broadcast journalist must achieve an interview that must not only contain relevant and interesting information, but looks and sounds good as well. The broadcast reporter faces a difficult task – getting people to talk concisely with clarity and confidence. If the interviewee is anxious or unsure about what is required they will not be spontaneous or clear in their answers.

Many people who are interviewed on television and radio may never have appeared on air before and have no idea what to expect. They can be nervous or may come across as defensive, brash or even aggressive. Often potential interviewees who talk with ease over the phone or off-camera will freeze when the camera or tape machine is switched on. It is the reporter's job to reassure them and to get the best out of the interview. Explaining what is going on and why, can help put the interviewee at ease and prevent them feeling quite so intimidated by the process.

Remember to introduce yourself, and your crew, if you are working for television. You want the interviewee to trust you, so be friendly. It is important to judge each situation individually. Sometimes it is important to be friendly and informal, other times to be authoritative and professional, and if you're dealing with the personal or emotional interview, sympathy and sensitivity are vital. A good interviewer will take control, they are the one asking the questions; they must be persistent and determined, but whatever the situation they must also always be polite and courteous.

Encourage your interviewee by maintaining eye contact, nodding and expressing sympathy or simply expressing interest in what they are saying, but not with audible or verbal expressions. Reassure the interviewee that if they lose track of what they are saying you can pause the interview and give them time to collect their thoughts. The radio reporter can also tidy up any coughs, stumbles or pauses in the edit.

Reporting for broadcast often means appearing or being intrusive. The reporter must be there, you must communicate with people face-to-face and that can mean thrusting a microphone or a camera at someone in the midst of a traumatic or tragic experience.

SOME BROADCAST DO'S AND DON'TS

Always check your equipment is working and adjust recording levels before proceeding with the interview.

Do your homework. There is nothing more unprofessional than turning up to an interview about which you know little or nothing. Make sure you get your facts right and do not say things which will make you look ignorant, foolish or unprofessional.

Don't write out your questions in full, make some brief notes about the key areas or issues you want to cover in the interview and commit them to memory. Using notes in interviews is distracting; particularly on television, and can give the impression that you don't know what you are talking about.

Don't allow your interviewee to do it either – it will make the interview feel dictated and artificial.

Do give the interviewee some idea of the issues or areas to be covered; it will help them collect their thoughts and prompt better answers from them. However resist the temptation to give the interviewee the questions in full, and don't rehearse the interview. The best interviews are those that are natural and spontaneous. Rehearsing the interview can lead the interviewee to omit important or interesting information once the tape is rolling because they will conclude they have already talked about it. It can also lead to them making references that make no sense to the audience, for example, 'As I said before ...'

What to ask

Questioning is particularly important in a broadcast interview because, not only might you want to include the questions in your final edited item, but good questions produce good answers, and articulate, thoughtful answers are essential for a recorded piece.

Interview questions should be simple, clear, concise and to the point. If the question is long winded or introduces too may issues at once the interviewee will be confused and unable to answer. The question must not be either too wide nor too narrow in scope. Remember you are asking questions, not making statements to be either confirmed or denied. The inexperienced reporter often makes the mistake of asking closed questions. What you want is explanation or comment; closed questions prompt a yes or no response: 'Councillor, will the new speed restriction measures cut the number of accidents on the estate?'

Put this way, the interviewee must offer more information: 'Councillor, *how* will the new speed restriction measures cut the number of accidents on the estate?'

Sometimes you may wish to prompt a yes or no answer, and therefore it makes sense to ask a closed question: 'Mr Kinnock, will you step down as party leader if Labour loses the general election next month?'

On the other hand do not ask questions that are too wide. The interviewee will not know where to start answering the question, or will be given so much scope they will not know where to stop. Imprecise questions not only allow the interviewee to ramble or publicise their cause they also use up tape and take longer to edit: 'You're opposed to the government's road-building programme. What do you think is wrong with their plans for the country's road network?'

Multiple questions are again too wide. The interviewee may forget to answer part of the question, or deliberately choose to answer only part of it: 'How were officers able to continue their campaign of harassment and intimidation of suspects for so long, despite concerns and repeated complaints from colleagues, and how will you stop this happening again in the future?'

If you don't ask a question, the interviewee will be unsure if, or how, they should respond.

Reporter: 'Mr Smith you're head teacher at St Thomas's Primary School. Only three years ago the school had a reputation for truancy, bullying and poor educational standards, today it's one of the best schools in the area. It's a remarkable transformation.'

Head: 'That's true, but what is your question?'

The Q & A

The reporter covering a breaking story may often find they sometimes become the interviewee. It may not yet be possible to grab eye witnesses or other contributors, but the reporter is available and can provide up-to-date information. Q & A stands for 'question and answer' and is a first-hand account of events from the scene. The questions will be scripted by the reporter as the presenter asking the questions is unlikely to be up-to-speed with developments at the scene, or may ask questions which the reporter cannot answer. It should contain interesting information and detail and should not degenerate into waffle or repetition.

GETTING THE STORY BACK

Television

Developments in technology have made it possible to feed material from even the remotest locations around the world in minutes. The television newsroom has at its disposal a number of ways of getting material back to base for transmission.

In regional operations the most obvious and the cheapest way is for the crew or reporter to deliver the tape by hand. However, if time is very tight or the reporter or crew are required to provide *rushes* (raw and uncut pictures) before going onto another job, a detour to the newsroom may not be possible or desirable. Many newsrooms hire motorcycle despatch riders to deliver tapes, some even directly employ their own couriers. Alternatively tapes can be sent from a fixed feedpoint, often an edit suite and/or studio facility located in the outreaches of the station's patch, or close to centres of government, industry or commerce where material can be fed via cable links to base.

A links vehicle or outside broadcast unit can also be used to provide location facilities for feeding material back to base. Most links vehicles have replay machines and a facility to transmit a signal either via microwave or satellite. They can send rushes material and play in live interviews, but are not equipped with editing facilities, unlike the OB unit. Once the links vehicle or the OB unit has been set up, material can be sent directly from location to base almost instantaneously. Not only does this save time but, on a breaking story, it means new information can be included in the programme even while it is on air.

Such facilities, however, can be costly to use. Links and OB units require extra specialist staff to operate them. It is not always possible to situate them in the required location. Microwave signals must have a clear line of sight to the receiver and can be blocked by high buildings, trees and hills. High tides can also prevent the signal getting through. This often means sending out the unit to do a reconnaissance prior to transmission. The vehicles are often cumbersome and slow because of the weight of the equipment and the curiosity of the public can often make live transmissions difficult.

Satellite circuits, usually booked in block time periods of about fifteen minutes, are expensive and cancellation charges are high. Satellite links can be affected by the weather, particularly rain and snow, and aircraft movement. The delay experienced when transmitting via a satellite link is a big drawback

– a delay of only two or three seconds during a live broadcast can seem like an age.

If the material if not urgently required, footage shot abroad can be sent back by air cargo.

Radio

The quickest and easiest way to get audio back to the radio station is via the phone or from the radio car. Most larger radio stations will have a car equipped with a radio transmitter mast from which the reporter can feed back actuality, interviews or voice-over material. Like the television links, vehicle and OB unit the signal must have line of sight to the transmitter and can be affected by high buildings and the topography of the location. They also have a fairly limited range.

For most smaller or local news stations use of ISDN lines is the other most common way of feeding broadcast quality audio via a high quality telephone line, usually situated in a studio or other feedpoint location. It stands for Integrated Services Digital Network and the cables eliminate the crackle of standard telephone lines.

Many larger operations are increasingly making use of satellite cars, for example most of the material used by BBC Five Live is now sent via satellite. The satellite dish is situated on the roof of the vehicle and it enables material to be sent from virtually any location. However, sending material in this way is expensive and it takes longer to rig the vehicle ready for transmission than the conventional radio car with its radio mast.

Journalists on some BBC network stations have recently adopted Scoop Reporter units as an alternative means of sending interviews and voicers to the station. Basically the unit, about the size of a laptop computer, can be simply plugged into an analogue phone or fax point and a 13 amp socket; a microphone and headphones are attached to the unit. The quality is not quite as good as an ISDN line but it is a simple and flexible way of feeding broadcast quality audio.

Library material, sound effects, music and graphics

The purpose of sound effects is to stir the imagination of the listener and to create a sense of place and time as a backdrop for a story. The over-use or inappropriate use of sound effects or music can become clichéd. Simple sounds, used occasionally and creatively, can make the difference between a formulaic, workmanlike feature and a memorable and inspired piece of radio. In particular, music that does not connect or relate to the story can easily create the wrong associations or tone, and can even offend or alienate the listener.

The television reporter has, in addition to the rushes material, a whole armoury of effects and extra visual material that can be used to enhance a story. The *picture* or *film library* will have a stock of tapes and programmes which are indexed and stored for possible future use in current stories, for example, shots of the last great storms in the south of England which could be included in a report about the recent floods caused by changing weather conditions.

TV stations will also have a stock of *still pictures* or *freeze frames* generally of leading political figures, celebrities and personalities. The use of *graphics* and computer-animated images has increasingly become part of the TV report. These may include maps, written text or figures to accompany and simplify complex information, or animated images to reconstruct crashes or explosions.

Supers, astons or *captions*, as they are variously known, can be flashed up on screen to give interviewees' names, profession or position, dates, locations, sources of material or other statistics.

Chromakey or *CSO* (colour separation overlay) is a means of electronically displaying still or moving pictures behind the newsreader. From the studio you will see only a very bright blue or green backdrop, which is replaced by the vision mixer with a graphic, or visual from a second camera.

11
Filing the story

Speed is vital when sending copy to your office. Often you need to file before you've even finished the story. When this happens, it needs to be made clear to those receiving it that this is the case. Often – such as filing the first quarter of a football match – it will be obvious, but at other times it may not be. Filing the first part of a story on a major house fire and then later adding the quotes from an interview with the fire chief and the fire victims is a sensible thing to do for an evening paper or radio station around deadline, but the newsdesk needs to know that that is what's happening.

HARD COPY

Although new technology in newsrooms has revolutionised methods of copy transmission, it is occasionally necessary to send copy to a newspaper or magazine by fax or through the post as hard copy (on paper).

You should always double space such copy, putting your name, the date of the copy and a numbered catchline at the top. Put 'mf' (for 'more follows') at the bottom of each sheet and 'ends' at the bottom of the final sheet. Under this put your name, address and phone numbers so that if subs have any queries they know who to contact and the accounts office knows where to send the cheque.

Figure 11.1 is an example of how hard copy should look. Note the catchline (in this case the word 'Reporting' and how it is numbered to show the page number):

If you are sending the file by floppy disk, then both the electronic copy and the floppy disk should be clearly marked with your name, address and phone number and, on the floppy disk, the name of the file.

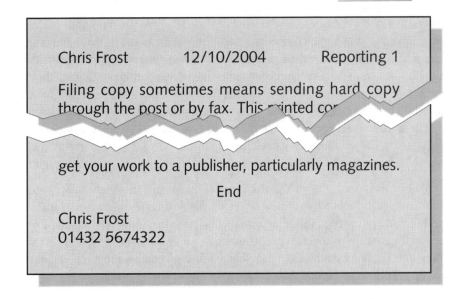

Chris Frost   12/10/2004   Reporting 1

Filing copy sometimes means sending hard copy
through the post or by fax. This printed co...

get your work to a publisher, particularly magazines.

End

Chris Frost
01432 5674322

Figure 11.1 Presentation of hard copy

PHONING COPY

You may also find yourself phoning copy through to a newsroom from time to time. Although it's relatively easy to attach your laptop to a phone line and FTP or e-mail copy, it may be that the connection is broken, or your mobile has run out of battery or you are trying to use a phone box. The one golden rule with technology is that, if it can break down, it will, and usually at the most inconvenient time. Once, I did actually have something go wrong with my car just as I was taking it in to be serviced, but it still didn't make up for all the times I've been stuck on a dark, lonely road with a car that won't go.

The traditional method of filing a story to a newspaper from outside the office is to find a phone box and read it over to a copytaker who types the story into the office copy system. Often this was done from a notebook with the reporter composing the story as he or she went along. Sometimes, if there was a bit more time available, the story could have been drafted in the notebook. Either way, if time is of the essence, don't re-transcribe quotes. Mark each quote in your notebook with a number and just put the number in your story. This will save quite a bit of time and allow you to get your copy in quicker. The mobile phone and laptop have made all this easier – but only when they work!

The art of copy filing is important. If the reporter is slow, the story may miss the deadline. If mistakes are made they could creep into the paper. One important tip to remember is to make friends with the copytakers. When the reporter is under pressure with a mobile that keeps losing signal or in a draughty phone box, with a queue of irate punters waiting outside to ring the bookies, it's easy to forget that the person on the other end of the phone is human too. Be polite, enunciate clearly and listen for their responses. Once contact is made with the copytaker the first instruction is to give them your name and the catchline of the story. If the story needs to be looked at by the office lawyer ask the copytaker to mark it clearly at the top for Legal Checks.

Then you can launch into filing the piece. Read it out in a clear voice, broken down into sections of around five or six words at a time, not whole sentences. The copytaker has to remember what you have just said as he or she types. They will generally tell you when they have completed each typed section, to enable you to move on to the next. But each copytaker adopts his or her own style, so you have to be adaptable too.

Each time you reach a word with a capital letter, you must tell the copytaker and spell out the word to avoid mistakes. All punctuation must be dictated too, including full stops at the end of sentences plus the end of paragraphs.

Filing figures accurately and clearly is a crucial part of copy filing, whether it's an age, an amount of money or the number of people in a crowd. The onus is on you to get it right and make sure the copytaker has taken it down correctly. Should you need to file a memo to the newsdesk or the subs be sure that you make this clear to the copytaker. File it separately and ask them to mark it clearly at the top as a memo to: whoever, from: whoever. The worst possible mistake would be to file a confidential memo, with background information, which crept into the paper because it was added on to the end of a story.

If you need to file extra copy on the same story later in the day, tell the copytaker that it is add-copy. File your name at the top of the piece and ask them to name the file 'add- (whatever the original catchline was)'. For this reason it is very important to remember what catchline you used first time round. It will be a time-consuming task for them to seek out your first story to find it for you.

The following is an example of how to file copy:

Sentence to be filed:

> When Mr Arthur Smythe returned to his £95,000 luxury home in Wythington Avenue, Preston it was surrounded by a crowd of 300 protesters, waving placards with the slogan 'End Animal Experiments'.

Method of filing:

> When Mr Arthur Smythe, cap A for Arthur – normal spelling, cap S for sugar, m-y-t-h-e [wait] returned to his pounds sterling, ninety five thousand, that's nine, five, comma zero zero zero luxury home [wait] in Wythington Avenue comma Preston, cap W, y-t-h-i-n-g-t-o-n Avenue, [wait] it was surrounded by a crowd of 300 that's three, zero, zero protesters, comma [wait] waving placards with the slogan [wait] open internal quotes, caps for start of each word, End Animal Experiments, close internal quotes, point, new par.

Spell out letters and figures that can be easily confused. An 'S' on the end of a poor phone link, may sound like an 'F' unless you say, 'S for sugar' or 'F for Freddie'. T and D are commonly transposed too, as are P and B, M and N. Nine and five are also easily misunderstood. Enunciate clearly and repeat if necessary. Copy-filing and copytaking is a time-consuming and exact art. But it's often the only method of transmitting a story in time for a deadline.

ELECTRONIC PRESENTATION

Most reporters these days will be filing from a laptop over the phone. This is not a problem if you are a staff reporter because the paper will ensure that whatever system you use is compatible. But freelances may find it more difficult. Unless you regularly file to the same newsdesk, in which case they should help you to set up a compatible system, the best bet is to e-mail the copy either as a message or as an attachment. If you send copy as an attachment, you need to be sure that the file type is compatible with the system used by the newsdesk. Unless the story is very long, you are probably better-advised to send the copy as part of the e-mail message, leaving the newsdesk to cut and paste the copy across to their system.

E-mail is now very cheap and easily available. It is possible to send group e-mails so that the same copy can be sent to several newsdesks – which may be useful to freelances filing on a non-exclusive basis – at virtually the same cost (and the same time) as sending one e-mail.

Although the costs of mobile phones are still higher than landlines (at the time of writing!) because e-mails are so fast, this is not really a consideration and rather than risk trouble using acoustic couplers to fit telephone boxes, etc., it is probably best to use your laptop connected to your mobile, rather than have a BT connector, to plug into a landline. This is only really worth doing if you are likely to spend some time logged onto the World Wide Web. It's still possible to fax copy of course, although it is difficult to imagine any newsdesk now that has fax but not e-mail. Radio and TV newsdesks are expecting audio and video feed as well as a report and so will have their own method of filing.

DEALING WITH THE OFFICE

It's always important to ring the office before sending copy, or to e-mail them as part of the copy e-mail to let the newsdesk know what you have done and what you intend to do next. They need to know if they should expect further copy, pictures, video or audio. They also need to know where they can contact you in order to discuss any problems with the copy.

Breaking stories

Sometimes a story needs to be filed as it is happening. Sports stories, major disasters and other breaking stories mean having to ensure that you get time away from finding the story in order to be able to file it or find yourself somewhere suitable in order to keep up a running report. If you are aiming for a newspaper or broadcast news bulletin, this is getting more and more difficult as technology increases your ability to publish. Whether for a radio bulletin or for the voracious appetite of an on-line web site or 24-hour news channel you may have to make time to send over a report. That is easier now with mobile phones. Just turn away from the story and send your copy by phone. For radio and TV, that may well be done with a live link. A time will be arranged and at that time the bulletin will switch to your outside broadcast link and your words and pictures will be transmitted direct to the waiting public. For radio this can be done by phone but TV still requires a more sophisticated link in order to send the video signal.

Although each bulletin needs to be treated as a separate, updated news item, you need to be sure that you repeat the essential information early on for people who have only just tuned in. The Hatfield train crash happened in day time and so the first many people would have heard of it was their radio in the car on the way home or the main news bulletin on the TV. On a story that's breaking as fast as this, a new nose or intro (the introductory paragraph of the story) is needed for those people who have already heard the news, but we don't want to confuse the new listeners and, so the main information needs to be added early on in the story.

AVOIDING DISASTER

Filing copy gives you your last chance to check that it is right. The modern newsroom is shedding sub-editors and the emphasis is more and more on reporters getting it right first time – so your watchword must be to check and check again. There are obvious things such as names and addresses that can be got right with only a modicum of care, but you also need to remember to check the rest of your facts.

Watch out for obvious slip-ups like using a name after you have promised that person anonymity. Have you also used the name of the victim or an innocent relative or friend of a criminal? Sometimes it is unavoidable but you must be certain you are only using the name in the public interest. The BBC covers this at length in its Producer Guidelines and the Press Complaints Commission also talks about it in its code of practice. This says that:

> The press must avoid identifying relatives or friends of persons convicted or accused of crime without their consent. Particular regard should be paid to the potentially vulnerable position of children who are witnesses to, or victims of, crime. This should not be interpreted as restricting the right to report judicial proceedings.
>
> (PCC Code of Practice, December 1999)

After Harold Shipman had been found guilty of killing more than a dozen of his patients, his wife Primrose was pictured by some of the press, but the pictures were much lower keyed than many stories about wives and husbands used in the past. Her name, and that of her son, were used, but the stories were commenting more about how her life had been destroyed and how the family had stood behind the doctor until the end. We have to consider the extent to which it was in the public interest to discuss how a woman could be taken in by a husband who, it turned out, was guilty of many murders.

The PCC and the BBC Producer Guidelines also advise that reporters should be careful about publishing names and addresses (see Chapter 5).

Defamation

Defamation is a complex subject, which I only intend to mention in the broadest terms, but getting it wrong could cost you and your editor a lot of money. You should always warn the news editor if you think what you have written may be defamatory.

The law takes the view that everyone is entitled to maintain a good reputation and enjoy the respect of their fellow citizens. If you damage the reputation of a person by writing something that 'tends to lower him in the estimation of right-thinking members of society generally or tends to make them shun and avoid him' (Carey 1999: 39) then they can sue you, seeking an apology and/or damages. There are two types of defamation: libel and slander. Since defamation in a permanent form is libel, it is usually an action for libel that journalists face. The Broadcasting Act 1990 made it clear that broadcast material would be subject to an action for libel. For a libel to be actionable, defamatory material about the plaintiff must be communicated to a third party. The plaintiff must be able to prove that any reasonable person would be able to recognise who he or she was from the defamatory article, so just because you didn't use a name or a title doesn't mean it can't be libel, although it is not possible to defame a class or group of persons unless a specific individual can be identified.

There are several defences against an action for defamation. They are:

Justification (or truth);
Fair comment on a matter of public interest;
Privilege – absolute or qualified;
Innocent dissemination;
Offer of amends; and
Apology.

(Carey 1999: 45)

The first three tend to be the main defences used by journalists. The first involves the journalist proving that the defamatory material is true. The burden of proof is on the journalist and the court will assume that the material is not true unless there is sound evidence to the contrary.

Fair comment is used to allow comment on matters of public interest. This includes everything from criticism of a football team or the production of a new play to the political career of a politician. Fair comment is not always an easy defence. First you have to prove that the comment is one of opinion not fact. The opinion must be based on true facts. It might be fine to comment that somebody's performance of Hamlet lacked power because he had not rehearsed enough as he was always in the pub, if you could prove he was always in the pub. Otherwise it might be better to content yourself with the view that his performance seemed to lack power.

In order to use fair comment as a defence the comment must be:

- on a matter of public record;

- recognisable as comment;

- based upon facts which are true or privileged;

- fair – as judged objectively; and

- must not be motivated by malice.

(Crone 1995: 29)

Another important defence against defamation is privilege. Proceedings of parliament and judicial proceedings attract absolute privilege. In other words, no matter what is said, the person saying cannot be sued. Unfortunately, our reporting of what was said attracts only qualified privilege. The main difference is that those with absolute privilege can be motivated by malice and still not be sued, while qualified privilege does not apply if malice is proved. With qualified privilege the media has protection from libel proceedings provided a fair and accurate report is given, and provided a letter or statement of explanation from the plaintiff was published by the defendant if requested.

Qualified privilege covers meetings, reports and decisions of parliament, the courts, local authorities, public meetings, sporting associations, associations of art, science, religion or learning, public inquiries, tribunals and public registers. In a decision by the House of Lords in November 2000, qualified privilege was extended to press releases from such meetings.

The Defamation Act of 1996 also introduced the idea of an offer of amends. An offer of amends allows a publisher to make a suitable correction of the statement complained of. By combining this with an apology and agreed compensation, the defendant could save himself from an expensive libel action. This offer of amends is not available if the publisher knew the article to be untrue and defamatory. An apology can be made that might persuade a litigant against action and certainly might limit any further damages.

Copyright

Copyright is your rights in the material you have written. Intellectual property rights and moral rights allow authors to control their property and determine who has the right to exploit it. It also prevents others infringing those rights.

The Copyright, Designs and Patents Act 1988 gave authors three moral rights:

- the right to be identified as the author;
- the right of the author to ensure work is not subjected to derogatory treatment;
- the right not to have work falsely attributed to one.

The intellectual property rights ensure that the copyright-holder (usually the author, but not always) has the right to control how the work is used and be paid for its use. The right for authors to be associated with their work and prevent alterations or misuse needs to be asserted by author (my moral rights over this book should be asserted on the frontispiece). However, if the work is produced by someone in the course of his or her employment, then copyright may be owned by the employer. This is a contentious area as it does not apply to freelances who may have a contract for services, but only to employees, whether full- or part-time, who have a contract of employment (Crone 1995:

106). Thus freelances are free to retain rights over any piece they have written, even after a paper uses it, unless they specifically agree to extend the publisher's rights. However, the first two rights (to be associated and to prevent derogatory treatment) do not apply to the reporting of current events.

The Act can give journalists rights over material they have produced unless it was in the course of their staff employment. This is a tricky area of law, but the reporter's contract of employment should make it clear where the dividing lines is. So if, for instance, a reporter on *The Times* were to write a whodunnit, then his contract of employment would not normally cover that, so while *Times* newspapers would own all his copyrights in articles written for *The Times*, if the book turned out to be a best-seller, it is the reporter who would own the valuable copyright.

Copyright protects a wide range of creative endeavours: writing, plays, films, speeches, photographs, pictures and sculptures to name a few. The media cannot just copy a photograph or a picture, a speech or an article without gaining permission from the copyright-holder.

There can be no copyright on facts, news, ideas and information – only their presentation. Copyright can be sold like any other property and so the ownership of it can be important. If you borrow a wedding picture from a woman whose husband has gone missing in newsworthy circumstances, you may need permission from the copyright-holder to publish it. If that is the woman, then her loan implies approval. But if the picture were a professional portrait, then the copyright might not be hers.

There are some protections journalists can use for what would otherwise be breaches of copyright.

Incidental inclusion: If, for instance, an artist was filmed being interviewed in a gallery and a picture by another artist could be seen in the background, the production company might be able to claim its inclusion was incidental.

Fair dealing: This is the defence journalists are most likely to depend on. In order to report the news, reporters consistently use small excerpts from speeches and other copyright work such as reports and statements. Provided the speaker has not prohibited its use, something you can take as read in a public meeting, you can reproduce sections of a speech with impunity provided it is a fair and accurate report. The same applies to criticism. If you wish to criticise a film, book, play or anything else, then provided the copyright-holder is credited, and the amount of the work shown is fair, it is allowed to use someone else's copyright work. The courts have also shown themselves willing to consider a defence of public interest, even though it is not included in the Act.

Data Protection Act

The Data Protection Act 1984 was designed to protect people from computer invasion of privacy. It was introduced at the start of the big computer revolution at the end of the 1970s. Computers had been a part of our lives for a decade or more, but they were still enormous and fantastically expensive mainframes that could only be afforded by banks and large institutions. Personal computers (PCs) were introduced in the very early 1980s and caught on quickly. It became clear that, in order to protect the privacy of people whose personal details were being gathered on computers, that an Act of Parliament was required. The Data Protection Act 1984 and then 1998 brought considerable protection from 'Big Brother'. The Act is built around eight Data Protection Principles that require the data to have been obtained lawfully, used only for the purpose it was gathered, not kept longer than necessary and kept reasonably secure from unauthorised access. The data also has to be accurate, up to date and the subject of the data has the right to check such data and ask for its erasure.

The 1998 Act widens the meaning of data from the old 1984 Act. The whole Act does not come into effect until 2007 and by that time even paper records will be covered. At the moment, if a reporter has sensitive material, then it might be better to keep it in a paper record form because access to it can then be refused. But when the full Act is implemented, there will be nowhere to put it. Any accessible record system or filing system will be covered by the Act and the information can be required by the subject. The new Act introduces the concept of *Sensitive Personal Data*. This is described by the Act as information about:

- racial origin;
- political opinions;
- religious beliefs;
- trade union membership;
- physical or mental health;
- sexual life;
- commission or alleged commission of an offence;
- any proceedings for an offence or alleged offence.

This new section has considerable impact on the work of a reporter. The morning calls, for instance, may tell of a major road crash. Neither the police nor the hospital is now able to give information about any living victims. If the victims don't give permission to release information, then it is up to a senior police officer to agree to release information if there is a good public interest reason. A senior officer may well decide that an accident involving the local MP who was on his way home from making a speech about safe driving is a story in the public interest, but he or she may not. Since the reporter does not know who is involved, he or she can't argue there is public interest. Nor is the hospital likely to give a condition report for the same reason. While this may well be a reasonable protection of people's privacy (did we always need to know that burglars stole a TV set from the home of Mr John Smith of . . . ?) it is also a limitation of the ability of the media to bring people the news.

The Act allows for special purposes that offer some exemption from the need to inform data subjects:

- journalism;

- artistic purposes;

- literary purposes.

Confidential information

Breach of confidence is being used more often these days to protect the secrets of corporations and rich individuals. Any leak of confidential information could be a breach of confidence and Lord Denning has already ruled that one should not take advantage of information disclosed in confidence. Whilst this rarely applies directly to journalists about stories they wish to publish, it may well apply to the source. Someone who believes his or her confidence is being breached can apply for an injunction to prevent publication. The Blairs did this when the *Daily Mail* first attempted to publish the memoirs of the former nanny to the Blair children. Any such injunction is enforced by the court and breach of it would be contempt. Once an injunction is in force with one newspaper, it applies to all the media.

There are three tests under the law to determine whether something breaches confidence:

- the matter must bear the appropriate quality of confidences;

- the circumstances must impose an obligation of confidence;

- an unauthorised breach must be detrimental.

The quality of confidence is tested by the court by asking if a reasonable man in the position of the defendant would have realised the information in his possession was confidential. An obligation of confidence can be found in a number of relationships such as employer/employee, doctor/patient or student/teacher, so someone who was seeking to reveal information about his or her employer could be breaching confidence as in the Blair case mentioned on the previous page. Although there is now legal protection for those who want to expose malpractice in their work place or elsewhere, that protection does not apply if they tell their story to the media.

If you are covering a story that requires a breach of confidence – maybe an employee is giving you a good story on their employer, you should make the person aware that they risk an action if their name is revealed, and you may need to promise them confidentiality if you think the story is worth it.

Protection from harassment

The Protection From Harassment Act was designed to protect people from stalkers, but of course it could be used against a particularly persistent journalist. The law says that a person must not pursue a course of conduct which amounts, or which he knows or ought to know amounts, to harassment of another. There is a public interest defence when investigating crime, but it is doubtful that that is intended to protect journalists.

12
What next?

Today's reporter has to be able to offer a newsdesk more than just the ability to follow instructions. Reporters need to be able to think up good story ideas and develop them into follow-up stories, features or other stories. This is particularly important for freelances, who need to come up with good ideas in order to ensure someone pays them the following week. Being creative about story ideas and their development is crucial. It is also something that you can develop in yourself after just a little thought and some practice.

WHAT IS CREATIVE THINKING?

Creativity is latent in almost everyone. In creativity the emotional and the non-rational parts of our mind are as important as the logical and the rational. Just as we can train our rational and logical mind to work better by educating it, so we can train our non-rational mind to be more creative by practice and education.

Creativity is often sparked by problem solving. For the journalist, the problem is: 'How do I find stories that will excite readers or viewers and how do I present the story in a way that will attract them to buy my newspapers/broadcasts and enjoy the experience of reading to the end?'

One of the things that often blocks our creativity is our own inhibitions. Psychologists believe we have a built-in censor that limits the information we are prepared to accept from the preconscious in order to protect ourselves from being overwhelmed by the information we contain in our brain. Filters appropriate to our situation ensure appropriate recollection. If we are in a leisure situation, leisure links are used and work recollections are unwelcome. If we are at work we do the opposite. This could well be the reason why an idea will come to us out of context. We might have been wracking our brain to consider how to extend a particular story, but as soon as we settle into a different activity, socialising with friends or watching TV, the idea comes to us. It seems that during the incubation phase of the idea, because we have adjusted the parameters of the censor, an association that we otherwise would not have considered will be delivered to our subconscious and our conscious mind will suddenly recognise it as appropriate for the problem we were dealing with before.

The way we work and are trained often seems to limit creativity. We come to fear expressing the weird and unusual because of peer pressure. If we are concerned that others will laugh at our ideas, we will not put our ideas forward, and if we never put ideas forward, we will probably stop having them at all. Creativity, imagination and good ideas are essential for success, particularly in journalism, although of course none of these is any good unless supported by hard work. And creative thinking is the hardest work of all, requiring intense discipline, concentration and planning.

Much of the creative thinking required of journalists is idea development. You've got a story idea but you need to develop it further – produce it as a series, perhaps, or build some background features. There are several techniques you can use.

Spider diagrams

These can be very useful for developing ideas. Write down the original idea and then spin out spider's legs to new ideas which then themselves spin out new ideas and so on. The disadvantage of spider diagrams is that after a few spiders have been drawn it is tempting to end the process before all the elements are thought through and you need to 'Beware the dangers of early commitment to an idea or strategy' (Raudsepp 1971: 114). There is an example of a spider diagram in Figure 12.1. Here I have chosen the Queen Mother's 100th birthday and expanded out from there with a number of ideas, each of which has spawned new ideas. See how I've included the concept of past, present and future as these often help develop ideas. I'm sure you could continue to develop further ideas of your own.

Brainstorming

Brainstorming was invented by Edward de Bono and given substance in his book, *Lateral Thinking* (De Bono 1977). He says we should always challenge assumptions. We often say we can't do something because that is the way it has always been. But technology can change things and what we want can change and that allows us to rethink and do the unthinkable. De Bono says we need to suspend judgement. Often we will discard an idea before we have thought it through because it sounds silly at first. Often developing the idea can change that view. Boring or clichéd ideas might be safe, but challenging,

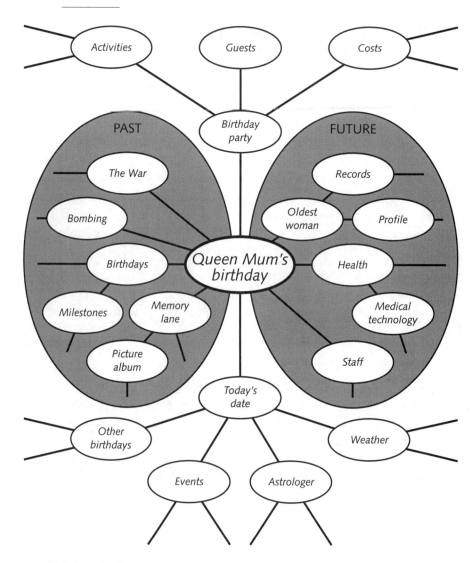

Figure 12.1 A spider diagram

unusual and exciting ideas are what newsdesks really want – and are prepared to pay for.

De Bono says that: 'The four rules of brainstorming in a group are: (1) Adverse criticism is taboo; (2) freewheeling is welcomed; (3) quantity is wanted; and (4) combination and improvement are sought' (Barron 1969: 132). Despite working best as a group activity, brainstorming can work even when you are on your own – provided you take it seriously and suspend judgement. You need to note down all your ideas in a formal session. In other words, you have to say to yourself that you will think about this idea for a solid ten minutes, writing down every idea you have. Ten minutes may not seem like a long time, but to concentrate on one idea for that length of time and brainstorm other ideas is very hard work. Ten minutes can seem like an age as you struggle to write down more and more bizarre ideas. But, provided you concentrate completely for this time you should come up with some excellent ideas based around the original spark to the story.

FOLLOWING UP A STORY

Once the initial story has been written that is not the end of it. Some stories obviously require following up. At the start of the Paddington rail crash for instance, it was clear that any reporter working on the story would be filing copy for each edition until the news editor decided otherwise and many reporters would have worked on nothing else for several weeks. Inevitably, though, the story would die away and the reporters were moved on to something else. In all such stories it is important to note likely key dates for follow ups in the diary. The anniversary and even ten-year anniversary are two obvious dates to pop into the diary for follow-up stories. The date of funerals, the inquiry and any other associated event should also be entered as potential follow-up stories.

Thinking about the timeline in a story is a good way of developing further story ideas. What happened in the past to lead to this story? What is likely to happen in the future – what are the consequences? In the case of the Paddington rail crash this would lead to a series of features and news stories about the fitting (or non-fitting) of train safety devices, other train crashes and how they link to this crash, and whether the government, the rail companies and other associated authorities have done enough in the past to prevent such accidents. The future brings us stories about the inquiry, how the survivors are coping, campaigns to improve rail safety and the effect such a major disaster has had on those working for the emergency services. Just a quick glance at this list shows the wealth of good story material available after this one incident and helps explain why you read so much about the Paddington rail disaster, its causes and its effects.

Pictures

It is also important that a good reporter thinks of picture ideas. When working with photographers, it is important to fully brief them about the story on which you are working. Photographers are the experts when it comes to pictures, but they can only be as good as the brief they receive. It also does no harm to suggest ideas to the photographer, so it is important that you think of picture ideas while you are working on the story. Not only can you then see if the photographer agrees with your idea, but you can also pass on other picture ideas to the newsdesk so that library or archive pictures can be included in the final package.

Using library pictures can be extremely useful, but there are potential problems. If you get a chance, check your library's picture file of the interviewee before you go on the interview. This means when you meet the person you can quickly tell if the photograph is recent or very dated. There is nothing worse than interviewing a fifty-year-old man about the death of his grand-daughter in tragic circumstances and then illustrating it with a picture of a sneering twenty-two-year-old protester with long hair and wildly unfashionable clothes. Finding out before makes it easy to alert the picture desk, or at least gives you a chance to ask the interviewee for an up-to-date picture. On the other hand, interviewing a couple on their golden wedding and finding you have a picture of their marriage day fifty years before can add a charming memory to a feel-good story.

Asking interviewees for pictures of loved ones involved in stories is standard practice. Try to ensure the picture is as up to date as possible. Only recently, a witness came forward with information in the Suzy Lamplugh case, years after Ms Lamplugh went missing. It seems that the picture the police used to seek witnesses had her pictured as a blonde, but in fact on the day of her death she was a brunette. Because of this, the witness did not put two and two together for years. Children change very quickly and you must try to get a picture as up to date as possible. The temptation is often to use the official school photographs that are taken every year in schools for parents to buy. Even if these are a couple of years out of date, parents will often prefer you to use one of these showing their child looking well groomed and well behaved. But often these pictures are not a very accurate reflection of the child and are dated. The copyright also belongs to the photographer and you may have to pay him or her for its use, unless the police have negotiated an arrangement. Better to use a holiday snap which will probably not be as good in terms of quality, but is more likely to be up to date and is certainly more likely to show some character.

When you borrow such a picture you must treat it with care. This is something the family will cherish and they will want it returned. Usually they will only let you have it on the promise of returning it. Some reporters borrow the family's whole picture album in an attempt to prevent other news media getting a picture. This puts an even heavier burden on the reporter who must make sure the pictures are returned or rob the family of precious memories – all they may have if the child has been killed. Your best bet is to take the picture to the photographic department and get it copied or scanned into the computer system while you wait. You can then take the picture and put it into an envelope that you can keep in a safe place. You can then personally return it in a day or two. The personal return ensures that the picture is not accidentally lost in the post, it also ensures that if there is any follow-up story, you will have a good reason to talk to one of the family and up-date your information.

Freelances

Freelances have particular requirements when it comes to developing stories. Not only do they need to think of good ideas for stories in the first place, but they also need to consider where they are going to sell the story. Some freelances specialise in an area of reporting and already have key markets lined up. This can be a good way to earn a freelance living. Perhaps you specialise in social work. This means finding news and feature stories in this field and sending them to the specialist magazines in this area. After a while these magazines will get to recognise the expertise of such a freelance and may offer commissions or ask the freelance to cover conferences or special events. Other non-specialist publications often have specialist pages. The *Guardian* for instance has its weekly education supplement and the editor of this will publish appropriate education pieces and will also come to trust regular freelances with suitable expertise.

General freelances have more opportunities for a wider range of writing but will often have to deal with news editors they don't know. Having written a story, it is even more important for such freelances to ensure that the story is written in a way that suits the market of the target paper, magazine or broadcast station. This could mean writing the same story in a dozen different ways. A woman protester fined for criminal damage after breaking into a local Army base and painting a tank bright pink in protest at arms sales to Indonesia would allow a good freelance to sell the basic news story to a number of outlets – the BBC, all the nationals, the local dailies and some of the foreign agencies. An interview with the protester would also be of interest to some of the women's magazines: 'How I stood up to be counted' or 'Women in the front line'. Some alternative lifestyle magazines might also be interested in the story on the basis of why she did it. It's probably stretching things a bit to try to sell the story to trade mags such as *Paint World*, but only because their budget's not big enough to pay for 'Dulux puts tank in the pink'. Stories about how she broke into an Army base or the practical problems of painting a tank might also appeal to some specialist mags (although probably too specialist to be able to pay much). They would need to be handled with care because of the security implications, but it would certainly be possible to build the story into a fun feature on 'Five crazy things to do after a night of lager' for *FHM* or *Loaded*.

A different approach, a new intro and new writing style can change an idea radically enough to allow the thinking freelance to sell the same basic story to a dozen different markets.

13
And finally . . .

Throughout this text we have tried to discuss issues of ethics and good professional practice as they have come up, but it is important that you should have an understanding of the codes of practice and guidance and how they apply to the media in which you work. This means the Press Complaints Commission code for newspaper and magazine reporters, Radio Authority and Broadcasting Standards Commission code for independent sector radio journalists, the BBC Producer Guidelines and the Broadcasting Standards Commission code for BBC journalists and the Independent Television Commission and the Broadcasting Standards Commission code for independent television journalists. Journalists working on web sites linked to a traditional media should follow the codes applying in that medium, while journalists on web sites that are completely independent would still do well to adhere to the general tenor of all the codes.

ORGANISATIONS WITH CODES OF PRACTICE

Press Complaints Commission

A body set up and funded by the newspaper industry to investigate complaints brought by readers and to decide whether they have breached the industry's code of practice.

The PCC has a hotline for complaints. It will also answer queries from editors seeking advice on whether stories they wish to run breach the code of practice. The chair of the Commission is Lord Wakeham, a former Conservative Chief Whip. Its Code of Practice is agreed by a committee of editors, but the commission itself is made up of sixteen members, the majority of whom are lay members not connected with the media in any other way. The journalism members are editors or senior journalists. Their Code of Practice is available on: www.pcc.org.uk.

Broadcasting Standards Commission

Set up under the Broadcasting Act 1996 to investigate and adjudicate on complaints brought by listeners and viewers about programmes on either radio or TV in both the independent and public sectors. Members are appointed by the Secretary of State for Culture, Media and Sport.

Their Code of Practice is on the web site at www.bsc.org.uk.

Independent Television Commission

A body set up by the Broadcasting Act 1996 to award franchises to independent TV companies and to control the conduct of those franchise holders. It has the authority to fine franchise holders or even remove the franchise for serious breaches. Members of the ITC are appointed by the Secretary of State for Culture, Media and Sport. Code of conduct and other information is on the web site: www.itc.org.uk.

Radio Authority

A body set up by the Broadcasting Act 1996 to award franchises to independent radio companies and to control the conduct of those franchise holders. It has the authority to fine franchise holders or even remove the franchise for serious breaches. Members of the Radio Authority are appointed by the Secretary of State for Culture, Media and Sport. Code of conduct and other information is on the web site: www.radio-authority.org.uk.

British Broadcasting Corporation

A body set up by the government to control public sector broadcasting. The Governors are appointed by the Secretary of State for Culture, Media and Sport and are responsible for ensuring broadcasting adheres to appropriate standards. The BBC's Producer Guidelines are on the web site at www.bbc.co.uk/info/bbc/acc_index.shtml.

National Union of Journalists

The TUC-affiliated union for journalists in the UK. It has approximately 34,000 members in newspapers, broadcasting, magazines, books, PR and freelance journalism spread throughout the UK, Ireland and continental Europe. Office collectives are called chapels and are led by Mother or Fathers of the Chapel.

It has its own code of conduct, agreed by the members. This is policed by the Ethics Council, a body that examines complaints sent to it by members or branches. If the council finds a member guilty of breaching the code of conduct it can reprimand the member or recommend to the National Executive Council that the person be fined up to £1,000, suspended from membership or expelled. Their code of conduct and working practices are available at: www.nuj.org.uk.

OTHER JOURNALISM ORGANISATIONS

National Council for the Training of Journalists

A cross-industry body made up of directors from the Newspaper Society, Guild of British Editors, National Union of Journalists and the Institute of Journalists. It validates newspaper journalism courses and sets exams for the National Certificate in journalism (www.nctc.co.uk).

Broadcast Journalism Training Council

A cross-industry body of broadcast employers organisations, the BBC and the National Union of Journalists that validates broadcast journalism courses (www.bjtc.org.uk).

Chartered Institute of Journalists

An organisation for journalists in the UK. It has approximately 800 members working mostly in newspapers, many of them stringers and part-timers.

Association of Journalism Educators

A UK-based association of lecturers involved in journalism teaching.

Presswise

A UK-based charity set up to help those who believe they are victims of an intrusive press. It aims to represent such people to the media and change how the media deals with such cases (www.presswise.org.uk).

European Journalism Training Association

A Europe-wide association of schools of journalism in higher and further education. Represents approximately sixty schools throughout east and west Europe (www.ejta.nl).

International Federation of Journalists

An international association of journalism trade unions representing the views of members to the United Nations, European Commission and other national and supra-national bodies. The NUJ is a member (www.ifj.org).

British Society of Editors

An association of editors, mainly of newspapers, but it is also open to editors in broadcasting (www.ukeditors.org).

Newspaper Society

An association of provincial newspapers. It lobbies on behalf of the newspaper industry as well as offering advice to individual newspapers. It has an excellent legal department (www.newspapersoc.org.uk).

Newspaper Publishers Association

A body representing the owners of national newspapers in the UK.

Press Association

A privately-owned news agency providing national and international copy to provincial newspapers throughout the country on a fee-paying basis (www.pa.co.uk).

Periodical Publishers Association

A body that represents publishers in the magazine field. It lobbies government and organises training for journalists and other staff (www.ppa.org.uk).

Glossary

Actuality: Interviews or sound recorded on location.
Aston (brand): A name for a type of electronic caption generator.

BJTC: Broadcast Council for the Training of Journalists; a cross-industry body overseeing journalism training.
Byline: Name of the author.

Caption: Words giving an explanation of a picture or graphic.
Catchline: Name of a piece of copy.
Chromakey (colour separation overlay, CSO): Way of replacing a single colour with a second image or picture.
Contacts: Someone who provides information.
Copy story: News story for broadcast without accompanying interviews or audio.
Copytaker: Person who inputs copy dictated over the phone.
Copytaster: Someone who selects copy for publication.
Credit: Payment by a newsdesk for information or copy.
Cutaways: An editing shot which allows shots or speech to be edited without an unsightly jump cut.

Death knock: Visit to the recently bereaved.
Doorstepping: The persistent pursuit of an interviewee.
Down the line: Audio or video feed via an outside source or cable link.

Embargo: Instruction on press release not to use until a specific date or time.

Freelance: Self-employed journalist.
Freeze-frame: Single static image.

General views (GVs): Wide shot to establish scene or location.

Hand-out: Written information from formal news sources.
Holding copy: Initial version of a story left by a reporter.

Intro: Introduction – first part of a story.

Kill (as verb): To decide not to publish part or all of a story.

Lead ('leed'): Main story on a page.
Looking space: Framing for interview which suggests presence of reporter.

Medium close up: Shot framed on subject to show head and shoulders.

NCTJ: National Council for the Training of Journalists; a cross-industry body overseeing journalism training.
Newsdesk: News executives.
Nibs: News in brief.
NS: Newspaper Society (Employers' body).
NUJ: National Union of Journalists (Employees' body).

OB: Outside broadcast.

PA: Press Association.
Package: Report comprising interviews (and/or actuality and sound effects) separated by narrative links.
Par: Paragraph – as in, 'Give me six pars on that'. Usually around 30 words.
Phono: Voice report via the telephone.
Piece to camera: Information given by a reporter on location where the reporter directly faces the camera.

Reuters: International news agency specialising in financial and political affairs.
Rushes: Raw, unedited video tapes.

Set-ups: Sequence of shots used to establish or introduce an interviewee.
Side-bar: Story to side of main story adding information or extra detail.
Slug: Copy identification information. Formerly a slug of type.
Soundbites: Extract or snatch of interview or actuality.
Spike: As verb. To decide not to publish a story.
Splash: Front page main story given major display treatment.
Standfirst: Standalone piece introducing story and often including a byline.
Still/still store: Still images generally of leading politicians, celebrities.
Stringer: Supplier of copy or news tip-offs. Often local amateurs.
Sub: Sub-editor.
Subbed copy: Copy passed by a sub-editor.
Super (caption): Title or caption superimposed or electronically generated over an image.

Talking heads: Expert contributors or authority figures.
Tip: Information from a contact (named or anonymous) leading on to a story.

Up to the wire: Late edit, working right up to the point of transmission.

Voice-over: Commentary recorded over pictures.
Voicer: Explanation, details of story by a reporter.

Wallpaper: Generic shots used to overlay complex narrative.
Wildtrack: Ambient sound recorded on location.
Wire: Agency copy.

Further reading

In addition to codes of conduct, many organisations offer guidance and advice on the reporting of issues from mental health and suicide to children and drugs abuse. Indeed there are now so many such guidebooks, that they could be combined to make a full book on their own! The NUJ, Presswise and the Society of Editors try to help journalists by issuing advice from time to time that includes the best on all these subjects.

Guidelines can be obtained from the NUJ, Presswise or the Society of Editors or on the web on the following issues: Writing about race; Disability; Children; Refugees; Drug abuse; Mental health; Suicide; Age discrimination; AIDS; Sexuality; Court reporting; Local government; ACPO guidelines.

RECOMMENDED BOOKS

There are plenty of books about on journalism, but some are more useful than others. Below is a short critique of several books that I have found to be particularly useful over the years.

Carey, P. (1999) *Media Law* (2nd edn), London: Sweet and Maxwell. A well-rounded look at the law as it affects journalists written in layman's terms. Up to date, it covers the Human Rights Act, the new Data Protection Act as well as the main source of concerns for most journalists: defamation, copyright and contempt of court.

De Burgh, H. (2000) *Investigative Journalism*, London: Routledge. A series of essays about investigative journalism.

Evans, H. and Gillan, C. (1999) *Essential English for Journalists, Editors and Writers*, London: Pimlico. A reprinting of Harry Evans' classic guide to writing for newspapers. A must on every journalist's desk, this accessible guide should help you to improve your writing style.

Feeney, R. (2000) *Essential Local Government 2000* (9th edn), London: LGC Information. A detailed, up-to-date and easy to access guide to local government, its duties, powers and structures. It has a companion guide to central government.

Frost, C. (2000) *Media Ethics and Self-Regulation*, Harlow: Longman. This is a basic primer on the need for ethics in the media and how they are applied to the day-to-day professional lives of journalists. It also explains how the various self-regulatory bodies work.

Hicks, W. (1993) *English for Journalists*, London: Routledge. A good primer on English for journalists and others who want to be able to communicate well. Encourages a stylish and accurate approach to the use of English without being dogmatic.

Hicks, W. (1999) *Writing for Journalists*, London: Routledge. A very good book on how to write news and features for publication. Mainly interested in reporting for newspapers and magazines, it does not cover very much for broadcast.

Keeble, R. (2001) *The Newspapers Handbook* (3rd edn), London: Routledge. This book offers sound advice on reporting and writing aimed specifically at newspaper journalists.

Markham, U. (1993) *Dealing With Difficult People*, London: Thorson. A very readable book that gives useful guidance on dealing with different types of people. While aimed at a general audience, there is much here that is useful in any profession or trade that involves a lot of interaction with different types of people.

Northmore, D. (1996) *Lifting the Lid: a Guide to Investigative Research*, London: Cassell. A good introduction to some of the special skills of the investigative researcher.

O'Kane, B. (ed.) (1993) *Essential Finance for Journalists*, London: Price Waterhouse. Good advice and guidance on the financial maze that faces the journalist whether dealing with company accounts, the stock market or the personal finance nightmares of pensions, insurance and taxation.

Randall, D. (2000) *The Universal Journalist* (2nd edn), London: Pluto Press. A good all-round primer on reporting and writing. It covers the task of the journalist (mainly aimed at newspaper reporting) from start to finish.

Spark, D. (1998) *Journalist's Guide to Sources*, Oxford: Focal Press. A good reference book of sources in the UK.

Welsh, T. and Greenwood, W. (1999) *McNae's Essential Law for Journalists* (15th edn), London: Butterworths. This is excellent for print journalists but not so detailed about broadcast. It is worth checking you have the latest edition of these as, inevitably, the law changes regularly. Because of this, web sites can be useful and there are several that are designed to help journalists in this way (see Chapter 13 for useful sites). The Society of Editors and the Newspaper Society are particularly good in this respect.

Wilson, J. (1996) *Understanding Journalism*, London: Routledge. This also explores the kind of issues journalists face in their everyday lives in an easy-to-read form, well structured, making it an easy-to-use reference book.

Internet sites of interest

GOVERNMENT AND POLITICS

- UK Parliament: **http://www.parliament.uk** (ideal for parliamentary business, MPs, government ministers, Hansard, etc.).

- Central Office of Information: **www.coi.gov.uk**. Press releases for all government departments.

- Government portal site: **www.open.gov.uk**.

- Information from local government: **www.local-government.net**.

- The Prime Minister's site: **www.number-10.gov.uk**.

- The Department of National Heritage: **http://www.heritage.gov.uk**. Press releases on media issues.

- Foreign and Commonwealth Office: **http://www.fco.gov.uk/travel**. Up-to-date travel and visa information on the countries of the world.

- Labour Party: **www.labour.org.uk**.

- Conservative Party: **www.conservatives.com** or **www.conservative-party.org.uk**.

- Liberal Democrats: **libdems.org.uk**.

- Register of political parties: **www.party-register.gov.uk**.

- Statistics: **www.statsbase.gov.uk**.

- Local councils can be found on **www.local-government.net**.

- Information on quangos: **www.cabinet-office.gov.uk/quango**.

ORGANISATIONS

- The Suzy Lamplugh Trust: **www.suzylamplugh.org**.

- Trades Union Congress (has links to most affiliated unions): **www.tuc.org.uk**.

- Companies House: **www.companies-house.gov.uk**.

- Insolvent companies: **www.insolvency.co.uk**.

INFORMATION

- **www.business.knowledge.com**.

- BT phone directories: **www.bt.com**.

- Maps: Search for suitable map in directory.

MEDIA

- BBC news and information including producer guidelines: **www.bbc.co.uk** (BBC Producer Guidelines: **www.bbc.co.uk/info/bbc/acc_index.shtml**).

- Open Media Research Institute: **www.omri.cz/index.html**.

- Journalism sources:
  - **www.holdthefrontpage.co.uk**
  - **www.octopod.demon.co.uk/journ_UK.htm**
  - **www.newsdesk.co.uk**
  - **www.fair.org**
  - **markovits.com/journalism/jlinks.shtml**
  - **www.pewcenter.org**

- European journalism: **www.demon.co.uk/eurojournalism/**.

- Broadcasting Standards Commission: **www.bsc.org.uk**.

- Broadcast Journalism Training Council: **www.bjtc.org.uk**.

- Campaign for the Protection of Journalists: **www.cpj.org**.

- Periodical Publishers Association: **www.ppa.co.uk**.

- Skillset (broadcasting training organisation): **www.skillset.org.uk**.

- Independent Television Commission: **www.itc.org.uk**.

- Press Complaints Commission: **www.pcc.org.uk**.

- National Union of Journalists: **www.nuj.org.uk**.

- National Council for the Training of Journalists: **www.nctj.co.uk**.

- Reporters Sans Frontières: **www.rsf.org**.

- International Federation of Journalists: **www.ifj.org**.

- European Journalism Training Association: **www.ejta.nl**.

- British Society of Editors: **www.ukeditors.org**.

- Newspaper Society: **www.ns.org.uk**.

- University of Central Lancashire, Department of Journalism: **www.uclan.ac.uk/facs/lbs/depts/journ/index.htm**.

- University of Aberystwyth: **www.aber.ac.uk**.

- Bournemouth University: **www.bournemouth.ac.uk**.

- Cardiff University: **www.cf.ac.uk/jomec**.

- City University: **www.jour.city.ac.uk/~neilt/journo/main.html**.

- Falmouth College of Art and Design: **www.fcad.ac.uk**.

- Napier University: **www.napier.ac.uk**.

- Nottingham Trent University: **www.ntu.ac.uk**.

- Presswise: **www.presswise.org.uk**.

- European codes of conduct can be found at: **www.uta.fi/ethicnet/**. Variety of different European ethics codes.

Don't forget that many of your local councils, organisations and businesses are now on the Net and that a quick search may well provide you with all the background information you need.

Search tips: Try typing in the company or organisation name followed by *co.uk* for a commercial organisation or *org.uk* for a charity or voluntary group. *Gov.uk* should be used for local or national government.

Example: There is a local company called *Acme tyres*. Try typing into your browser *www.acmetyres.co.uk*. You may go straight to their web site. If this fails, then use a search engine such as **yahoo.com**, **altavista.com** or **google.com**. Limit the search to the UK and then type in the name. If you are looking for a company then you must put the name in quotes 'Acme Tyres' for instance. If you are looking for sites about tyres then just type in: *tyres*. If you want to narrow the search to car types then type in *car+tyres* and the search engine will find documents that contain the words *car* and *tyres*. Don't forget, that if you are searching on a US site, that you would need to spell the word *tires*. Some of the better search engines offer these kinds of alternative search words for you to select.

Bibliography

Adair, S. (1999) *Press and Broadcast Media*, East Grinstead: Bowker Saur.

Allport, G.W. and Postman, L. (1947) *The Psychology of Rumor*, New York: Holt, Rinehart and Winston.

Anthony, S. (1973) 'Anxiety and rumor', *Journal of Social Psychology* 40, 3: 597–620.

Argyle, M. (1969) *Social Interaction*, London: Tavistock Publications.

Argyle, M. (1988) *Bodily Communication*, 2nd edn, London: Routledge.

Bagnall, N. (1993) *Newspaper Language*, Oxford: Focal Press.

Barker, M. and Petley, J. (1997) *Ill Effects*, London: Routledge.

Barron, F. (1969) *Creative Person and Creative Process*, New York: Holt, Rinehart and Winston.

Barthes, R. (1993) *Mythologies*, London: Vintage.

BBC (1999) *The Changing UK*, London: BBC.

BBC (2000) *BBC Producer Guidelines*, BBC, London. World Wide Web URL: http://www.bbc.co.uk/info/editorial/prodgl/contents/html.

Beaman, J. (2000) *Interviewing for Radio*, London: Routledge.

Bell, M. (1998) 'The journalism of attachment', in Kierans, M. (ed.) *Media Ethics*, London: Routledge.

Boyd, A. (1997) *Broadcast Journalism*, 4th edn, Oxford: Butterworth Heinemann.

Brett, M. (1988) *How To Read the Financial Pages*, London: Hutchinson.

Calahan, C. (1999) *A Journalist's Guide To The Internet*, Boston: Allyn and Bacon.

Carey, P. (1999) *Media Law*, 2nd edn, London: Sweet and Maxwell.

Chantler, P. and Harris, S. (1997) *Local Radio Journalism*, Oxford: Focal Press.

Corbett, B. (ed.) (1990) *Danger: Journalists At Work*, London: International Federation of Journalists.

Coupland, N., Giles, H. and Wiemann, J.M. (eds) (1991) *Miscommunication and Problematic Talk*, London: Sage.

Crone, T. (1995) *Law and the Media*, Oxford: Focal Press.

Curran, J. and Seaton, J. (1997) *Power Without Responsibility*, 3rd edn, London: Routledge.

Curtis, L. and Jempson, M. (1993) *Interference on the Airwaves*, London: CPBF.

Davis, A. (1979) *Working in Journalism*, London: BT Batsford.

Davis, A. (1988) *Magazine Journalism Today*, Oxford: Focal Press.

De Bono, E. (1986) *Six Thinking Hats*, London: Viking.

De Bono, E. (1977) *Lateral Thinking*, Harmondsworth: Penguin.

DeBurgh, H. (2000) *Investigative Journalism*, London: Routledge.

De Fleur, M. (1997) *Computer-Assisted Investigative Reporting*, Mahwah: Lawrence Erlbaum Associates.

Dobson, C. (1992) *The Freelance Journalist*, London: Butterworth/Heinemann.

Evans, H. and Gillan, C. (1999) *Essential English for Journalists, Editors and Writers*, London: Pimlico.

Feeney, R. (2000) *Essential Local Government 2000*, 9th edn, London: LGC Information.

Feldman, T. (1996) *An Introduction To Digital Media*, London: Routledge.

Fletcher, W. (1992) *Creative People*, London: Century Hutchinson.

Fowler, R. (1999) *Language in the News*, London: Routledge.

Franklin, B. (1997) *Newszak and News Media*, London: Arnold.

Franklin, B. and Murphy, D. (eds) (1998) *Making the Local News*, London: Routledge.

Franklin, B. and Murphy, D. (1998) 'Changing times: local newspapers, technology and markets', in Franklin, B. and Murphy, D. (eds) *Making the Local News*, London: Routledge.

Fromkin, V. and Rodman, F. (1993) *An Introduction to Language*, Fort Worth: Harcourt Brace.

Frost, C. (2000) *Media Ethics and Self-Regulation*, Harlow: Longman.

Fuller, J. (1996) *News Values*, Chicago: University of Chicago Press.

Gabriel, J. (1998) *Whitewash: Racialized Politics and the Media*, London: Routledge.

Galtung, J. and Ruge, M. (1997) 'The structure of foreign news', in Tumber, H. (1999) *News: A Reader*, Oxford: OUP.

Gans, H. (1980) *Deciding What's News*, London: Constable.

Garrand, T. (1997) *Writing for Multi-media*, Oxford: Focal Press.

Gluckman, M. (1963) 'Gossip and scandal', *Current Anthropology* 4, 3, June.

Goldie, F. (1985) *Successful Freelance Journalism*, Oxford: OUP.

Golding, P. and Elliott, P. (1979) *Making the News*, London: Longman.

Greenwood, W. and Welsh, T. (2001) *McNae's Essential Law For Journalists*, 6th edn, London: Butterworth Heinemann.

Gudykunst, W. (1994) *Bridging Differences*, Thousand Oaks: Sage.

Hachten, W. (1998) *The Troubles of Journalism*, London: LEA publishers.

Halberstam, J. (1992) 'A prolegomenon for a theory of news', in Cohen, E.D. (ed.) *Philosophical Issues in Journalism*, Cambridge: Harvard University Press.

Harris, G. and Spark, D. (1993) *Practical Newspaper Reporting*, Oxford: Focal Press.

Hart, A. (1991) *Understanding Media*, London: Routledge.

Hartley, J. (1982) *Understanding News*, London: Routledge.

Hausmann, C. (1987) *The Decision-making Process in Journalism*, Chicago: Nelson-Hall.

Henley, N. and Kramarae, C. (1991) 'Gender, Power, and Miscommunication', in Coupland, N., Giles, H. and Wiemann, J.M. (eds) *'Miscommunication' and Problematic Talk*, London: Sage.

Hennessy, B. and Hodgson, F.W. (1995) *Journalism Workbook*, Oxford: Focal Press.

Hicks, W. (1993) *English for Journalists*, London: Routledge.

Hicks, W. (1999) *Writing for Journalists*, London: Routledge.

Hoch, P. (1974) *The Newspaper Game*, London: Calder and Boyers.

Hodgson, F.W. (1993) *Modern Newspaper Practice*, Oxford: Focal Press.

Hodgson, F.W. (1998) *New Sub-editing*, Oxford: Focal Press.

Hoffman, A. (1992) *Research for Writers*, London: A&C Black.

Hopper, R. (1992) *Telephone Conversation*, Bloomington: Indiana University Press.

Houston, B. (1999) *Computer-assisted Reporting*, 2nd edn, New York: St Martins.

Huff, D. (1954) *How To Lie With Statistics*, London: Penguin.

Husband, C. (1975) *White Media Black Britain*, London: Arrow.

Jensen, K. (1998) *News of the World*, London: Routledge.

Jones, G. (1987) *The Business of Freelancing*, London: BFP.

Keeble, R. (1998) *The Newspapers Handbook*, 2nd edn, London: Routledge.

Keene, M. (1995) *Practical Photojournalism*, London: Focal Press.

Kieran, M. (1998) *Media Ethics*, London: Routledge.

Knapp, M. and Hall, J. (1997) *Nonverbal Communication in Human Interaction*, Fort Worth: Harcourt Brace.

Koch, T. (1990) *News as Myth*, Greenwood Press: NY.

Koch, T. (1991) *Journalism in the 21st Century: Online Information, Electronic Databases and the News*, Twickenham: Adamantine Press.

Laakaniemi, R. (1995) *Newswriting in Transition*, Chicago: Nelson Hall.

Lacey, N. (1998) *Image and Representation*, London: Macmillan Press.

Langer, J. (1998) *Tabloid Television*, London: Routledge.

Lorenz, A. and Vivian, J. (1996) *News Reporting and Writing*, Boston: Allyn and Bacon.

Markham, U. (1993) *How to Deal With Difficult People*, London: Thorsons.

Matelsk, M.J. (1991) *TV News Ethics*, London: Focal Press.

McGuire, M., Stilborne, L., McAdams, M. and Hyatt, C. (1997) *The Internet Handbook for Writers, Authors and Journalists*, London: Folium.

McLeish, R. (1999) *Radio Production*, 4th edn, Oxford: Focal Press.

McNair, B. (1999) *News and Journalism in the UK*, 3rd edn, London: Routledge.

Milroy, L. (1980) *Language and Social Networks*, Oxford: Basil Blackwell.

Moeller, D. (1999) *Compassion Fatigue*, London: Routledge.

Murphy, D. (1976) *The Silent Watchdog*, London: Constable.

Negrine, R. (1994) *Politics and the Mass Media In Britain*, London: Routledge.

Niblock, S. (1996) *Inside Journalism*, Blueprint.

Northmore, D. (1996) *Lifting the Lid*, London: Cassell.

NUJ (2000) *Rule Book*, London: NUJ.

O'Kane, B. (ed.) (1993) *Essential Finance for Journalists*, London: Price Waterhouse.

O'Malley, T. (1994) *Closedown*, London: Pluto Press.

Palmer, F. (1990) *Grammar*, London: Penguin.

Parsigian, E. (1996) *Proposal Savvy*, Thousand Oaks: Sage.

Philo, G. (ed.) (1996) *Media and Mental Distress*, Glasgow: Glasgow Media Group.

Press Council (1953–90) *The Press and the People. Annual Report of the Press Council*, London: Press Council.

Press Council (1991) *Press at the Prison Gates. Press Council Booklet no. 8*, London: Press Council.

Press Complaints Commission (1991–2001) *Report no. 1–52*, London: PCC.

Randall, D. (1996) *The Universal Journalist*, London: Pluto Press.

Raudsepp, E. (1971) 'Try these six steps to more ideas', in Davis, G. and Scott, J. (eds) *Training Creative Thinking*, New York: Holt, Rinehart and Winston.

Reah, D. (1998) *The Language of Newspapers*, London: Routledge.

Robertson, G. (1983) *People Against the Press*, London: Quartet.

Rosenblum, M. (1993) *Who Stole The News?*, New York: John Wiley.

Rosnow, R. and Fine, G. (1976) *Rumor and Gossip: The Social Psychology of Hearsay*, New York: Elsevier.

Royal Commission on the Press (1949) London: HMSO.

Schlesinger, P. (1978) *Putting Reality Together: BBC News*, London: Constable.

Schlesinger, P. and Tumber, H. (1994) *Reporting Crime: The Media Politics of Criminal Justice*, Oxford: Clarendon Press.

Searle, C. (1989) *Your Daily Dose – Racism and the Sun*, London: CPBF.

Sellers, L. (1968) *Doing it in Style*, Oxford: Pergamon Press.

Sellers, L. (1968) *Simple Subs Book*, Oxford: Pergamon Press.

Shibutani, T. (1966) *Improvised News*, Indianapolis: Bobbs-Merrill.

Smith, G. (1986) *Local Government for Journalists*, London: LGC Communications.

Spark, D. (1998) *Journalists' Guide to Sources*, Oxford: Focal Press.

Stokes, J. and Reading, A. (eds) (1999) *The Media in Britain*, London: Macmillan.

Taylor, J. (1999) *Body Horror*, Manchester: Manchester University Press.

Tomalin, N. (1997) 'Stop the press I want to get on', in Bromley, M. and O'Malley, T. (eds) *A Journalism Reader*, London: Routledge.

Tumber, H. (1999) *News: a Reader*, Oxford: OUP.

Venables, J. (1993) *What is News?*, Huntingdon: ELM Publications.

Ward, G. (1997) *Mental Health and The National Press*, London: Health Education Authority.

Waterhouse, K. (1989) *Waterhouse on Newspaper Style* London: Penguin.

Watson, J. (1998) *Media Communication*, London: Routledge.

Webbink, P. (1986) *The Power of the Eyes*, New York: Springer Publishing Co.

Welsh, T. and Greenwood, W. (1995) *Essential Law for Journalists*, 15th edn, London: Butterworths.

Whitaker, B. (1981) *News Limited: Why You Can't Read All About It*, London: Minority Press Group.

White, T. (1996) *Broadcast News Writing, Reporting and Producing*, 2nd edn, Boston: Focal Press.

Williams, F. (1957) *Dangerous Estate: The Anatomy of Newspapers*, Cambridge: Patrick Stephens.

Williams, F. (1969) *The Right To Know: The Rise of the World Press*, London: Longman.

Wilson, J. (1996) *Understanding Journalism*, London: Routledge.

Winston, B. (1998) *Media, Technology And Society*, London: Routledge.

Yorke, I. (1997) *Basic TV Reporting*, 2nd edn, Oxford: Focal Press.

Index